Gen STOP IT!
Uniting Generations

Bridging Generations for Mutual Growth,
Success, and Prosperity

Oreste J. DAversa, CPC

Life Coach

PUBLISHER'S NOTE

This book is designed to provide accurate and authoritative information. information in regard to the subject matter covered. It is sold with the understanding that neither the author nor publisher is engaged in rendering psychological, legal, or other professional service. If psychological, legal, professional advice or other expert assistance is required, the services of a professional in that field should be sought. The principles and concepts presented in this book are the opinions of the author and are based on his interpretations of the aforementioned principles. Neither the author nor publisher is liable or responsible to any person or entity for any errors contained on this book, or website, or for any special, incidental, or consequential damage caused or alleged to be caused directly or indirectly by the information contained on this book or website. Any application of the techniques, ideas, and suggestions in this book is at the reader's sole discretion and risk.

No part of this publication may be reproduced, redistributed, taught, stored in a retrieval system, or transmitted, in any form, or by any means, electronic, mechanical, photocopy, recording, or otherwise, without the prior written permission of the publisher.

Disclosure Statement: This book contains both AI-assisted and AI-generated content. The AI-assisted content was developed using tools to aid in brainstorming, editing, and refining the text, while the AI-generated content includes sections of the book created entirely by artificial intelligence. All AI-generated content has been reviewed and edited to ensure it meets the high standards of quality and originality.

FIRST EDITION

ISBN: 978-1-952294-38-9

Library of Congress Control Number: 2024915507

Published by: Cutting Edge Technology Publishing

Table of Contents

THIS

PAGE

INTENTIONALLY

LEFT

BLANK

About The Author

Oreste J. DAversa (O-rest-ee DA-versa), CPC
(Certified Professional Coach) is a Life Coach,
Career/Job Search Coach, and
College Major Coach **(www.CollegeMajorCoaching.com).**
He is the owner of Metropolitan Small Business Coaching LLC
(www.MetroSmallBusinessCoaching.com)
as a Business Coach, Consultant, and Trainer.
He is an Inter-Faith (All-Faiths) Minister
(www.GodLovesYouAndMe.org) ordained by
The New Seminary in New York City, New York.
He appears on podcasts, radio, and television programs
discussing his expertise in business-related and
personal development subjects.

He is the author of the following books:

- **Hey World! Why do I Feel All Alone in a Planet Full of People?**

- **UNPLUGGED! A Practical Guide to Managing Teenage Stress in the Digital Age**

- **AI, Robots and Humans: Our Servants or Masters?**

- **Life Beyond the Pandemic: A Practical New Journey Handbook**

- **The Resume and Cover Letter Writing Toolkit for the Successful Job Seeker**

- Power Interviewing: Proven Job Interview Techniques That Get You Results!

- The Step-by-Step Business Networking Kit: The Ultimate Business Networking System that Delivers Superior Results!

- SELL More Technology NOW!

- Selling for Non-Selling Professionals©

- Baby Boomer Entrepreneur: Implementing the Boomer Business Success System ®: The Complete and Proven Guide to Starting a Successful Business, having Financial Freedom with the Lifestyle that You Want

- Discovering Your Life Purpose: The Journey Within - The True Guide to Achieving Unlimited Happiness, Prosperity and Personal Fulfillment

- The Seven Simple Principles of Prosperity: Practical Exercises to Achieve a Rich, Happy and Joyous Life

- I Didn't Get a Chance to Say Good-bye ... Now What Can I Do?

- Write Your Own Funeral Service

- Healing the Holes in My Soul!: How I Saved My Own Life, Became Whole to Lead a Happy, Fulfilling and Joyous Life!

PREFACE

In today's rapidly evolving world, we find ourselves at a unique crossroads. The pace of technological advancement, societal change, and economic shifts has created a dynamic landscape unlike any other in human history. While these changes bring unprecedented opportunities, they also pose significant challenges, particularly in how different generations interact, collaborate, and coexist. As a self-help author, I have dedicated my career to exploring the intricacies of human relationships and the ways in which we can foster deeper connections and understanding. This book, *Gen STOP IT! Uniting Generations: Bridging Generations for Mutual Growth, Success, and Prosperity,* is a culmination of that work.

The idea for this book was born out of conversations, observations, and reflections on the generational divides that seem to grow wider with each passing year. Whether it's the Silent Generation, Baby Boomers, Generation X, Millennials, or Generation Z, each cohort has its own distinct set of experiences, values, and perspectives. These differences, while enriching, can also lead to misunderstandings, conflicts, and missed opportunities for collaboration and growth.

In writing this book, my aim is to offer a comprehensive guide to bridging these generational gaps, fostering mutual respect, and creating a more cohesive and harmonious society. The journey begins with understanding the interconnectedness of generations. We are not isolated entities but part of a continuum that spans time and space. Our histories, traditions, and innovations are interwoven, and recognizing this interconnectedness is the first step toward building stronger, more resilient communities.

Throughout this book, we will explore the power of the past and how historical contexts shape our present interactions. We will delve into the concept of bridging the gap, examining the ways in which we can overcome stereotypes, biases, and misunderstandings. The digital natives—those who have grown up in the age of the internet—will be a focal point of our discussion, as we seek to understand their unique worldview and the potential they hold for driving future progress.

Collaboration is a recurring theme in this book. We will look at the importance of collaborative success and how different generations can work together to achieve common goals. We will explore the symbiotic relationship between the experience of older generations and the fresh perspectives of the younger ones. Cultural and social synergy will be highlighted, emphasizing the importance of embracing diversity and fostering inclusive environments.

Economic interdependence is another critical area of exploration. As we navigate an increasingly globalized economy, understanding the economic ties that bind us is essential for collective prosperity. Emotional and psychological bonds are equally important. We will examine how empathy, compassion, and emotional intelligence can bridge generational divides and create deeper, more meaningful connections.

Finally, we will chart the path forward, offering practical strategies and insights for embracing our shared journey. The conclusion will tie together the themes of the book, underscoring the importance of unity and collaboration in achieving mutual growth, success, and prosperity.

Gen STOP IT! Uniting Generations is more than a book; it is a call to action. It is an invitation to look beyond our differences and recognize the strength that lies in our collective potential. Together, we can build a brighter future for all generations, fostering a world where mutual respect, understanding, and collaboration are the cornerstones of our shared success.

THIS

PAGE

INTENTIONALLY

LEFT

BLANK

Introduction: The Interconnectedness of Generations

In the grand tapestry of human existence, every thread is significant, each color meaningful. This intricate weave of generations—silent generation, baby boomers, Generation X, millennials, and Generation Z—forms the fabric of our collective history and shapes our shared future. In this book, Gen STOP IT! Uniting Generations: Bridging Generations for Mutual Growth, Success, and Prosperity, we delve into the essence of generational interconnectedness, exploring how we can harmonize our diverse experiences, values, and perspectives for mutual benefit.

The world we live in today is markedly different from the one our grandparents knew. The pace of technological advancement, societal evolution, and economic transformation has created an environment of unprecedented complexity and potential. With these rapid changes come opportunities for growth and innovation, but also challenges in maintaining cohesion and understanding among different generations. It is in this context that our journey begins—a journey to uncover the power of unity amidst diversity, to bridge the generational divides, and to foster a society where mutual respect and collaboration are paramount.

The Generational Divide

To understand the present, we must first look to the past. Each generation is a product of its time, shaped by the unique socio-economic, political, and cultural landscapes of its formative years. The silent generation, for example, grew up during the Great Depression and World War II, instilling in them values of hard work, resilience, and frugality. Baby boomers, born in the post-war era of prosperity, experienced significant social changes, including the civil rights movement and the sexual revolution, which influenced their ideals of freedom and self-expression.

Generation X, often referred to as the "latchkey" generation, navigated a world of increasing divorce rates and the rise of dual-income households, fostering independence and adaptability. Millennials, coming of age during the dawn of the internet and the Great Recession, value connectivity, inclusivity, and purpose-driven work. Generation Z, the true digital natives, have been immersed in technology from birth, shaping their outlook on communication, identity, and activism.

These generational differences, while enriching, can also lead to misunderstandings and conflicts. The silent generation may view millennials as entitled, while millennials might see baby boomers as out of touch with modern realities. Generation X may feel squeezed between caring for aging parents and supporting their own children, leading to stress and frustration. These tensions are natural but need not be divisive. By understanding the historical contexts and experiences that shape each generation, we can foster empathy and create a foundation for meaningful dialogue and collaboration.

The Power of Connectivity

In our quest to unite generations, we must leverage the tools at our disposal—most notably, technology. The digital revolution has transformed how we communicate, work, and connect with one another. Social media platforms, video conferencing tools, and instant messaging apps have made it possible to maintain relationships across vast distances and time zones. Yet, technology is a double-edged sword; while it can bridge gaps, it can also create echo chambers and exacerbate generational divides.

To harness the positive potential of technology, we must be intentional in its use. This involves creating inclusive digital spaces where all generations feel welcome and valued. For example, intergenerational mentorship programs can be facilitated online, pairing experienced professionals with younger individuals seeking guidance. Virtual communities can be established to share knowledge, experiences, and support. By fostering digital literacy among older generations and encouraging younger ones to appreciate the wisdom of their elders, we can create a more integrated and supportive society.

Bridging the Gap

The key to bridging generational gaps lies in fostering mutual respect and understanding. This begins with open, honest communication. Encourage conversations where different generations can share their stories, challenges, and aspirations. Create opportunities for intergenerational collaboration in the workplace, community projects, and educational settings. By working together, we can break down stereotypes and build a culture of inclusivity and cooperation.

Education plays a crucial role in this process. Schools and universities should incorporate intergenerational learning experiences, where students can engage with older generations to gain insights into history, culture, and life skills. Similarly, professional development programs should emphasize the value of diverse perspectives, promoting teamwork and innovation.

The Role of Leadership

Effective leadership is essential in guiding the integration of generations. Leaders must model the values of respect, empathy, and collaboration, fostering an environment where all voices are heard and valued. This involves recognizing and addressing biases, providing opportunities for intergenerational interaction, and celebrating the contributions of each generation.

Organizations that embrace intergenerational diversity are often more innovative and resilient. By tapping into the strengths of each generation, they can develop creative solutions to complex problems and adapt more effectively to changing circumstances. This approach not only enhances organizational performance but also contributes to the personal and professional growth of individuals.

Economic Interdependence

Economic interdependence is another critical aspect of generational interconnectedness. Each generation contributes to the economy in unique ways, and their collective efforts drive societal progress. For instance, older generations often provide financial stability and mentorship, while younger generations bring fresh ideas and technological expertise. By recognizing and leveraging these complementary strengths, we can create a more robust and dynamic economy.

Policies that support intergenerational cooperation, such as flexible work arrangements, lifelong learning opportunities, and social security systems that ensure the well-being of all age groups, are essential. These measures not only promote economic stability but also enhance social cohesion and trust.

Emotional and Psychological Bonds

At the heart of generational interconnectedness are the emotional and psychological bonds that unite us as human beings. Empathy, compassion, and emotional intelligence are vital in bridging generational divides. By cultivating these qualities, we can develop deeper, more meaningful connections with individuals from different generations.

Intergenerational activities, such as family gatherings, community events, and shared hobbies, can strengthen these bonds. Storytelling, in particular, is a powerful tool for connecting generations. By sharing our personal narratives, we can foster empathy, understanding, and a sense of shared identity.

The Path Forward

As we move forward, it is essential to embrace a mindset of continuous learning and adaptation. The world will continue to change, and new generations will emerge with their own unique challenges and opportunities. By fostering a culture of respect, collaboration, and mutual support, we can navigate these changes together and create a brighter future for all.

Gen STOP IT! Uniting Generations is a call to action. It is an invitation to look beyond our differences and recognize the strength that lies in our collective potential. Together, we can build a world where mutual respect, understanding, and collaboration are the cornerstones of our shared success. This book is a guide to that journey, offering insights, strategies, and inspiration for uniting generations and fostering a more cohesive and prosperous society.

Let us embark on this journey together, with an open mind and a compassionate heart, ready to bridge the generational divides and create a legacy of unity and prosperity for future generations.

Chapter 1: The Power of the Past

The power of the past is an undeniable force that shapes our present and informs our future. As we embark on our journey to unite generations, it is crucial to understand and appreciate the profound influence that history has on our lives. Each generation is a product of its time, molded by the significant events, cultural shifts, and societal norms of its formative years. By examining the past, we can gain valuable insights into the experiences, values, and perspectives of different generations, fostering empathy and mutual understanding.

Historical Contexts and Generational Identities

Every generation carries the imprint of its historical context. The silent generation, for instance, was born into a world of economic hardship and global conflict. The Great Depression and World War II instilled in them a sense of resilience, duty, and frugality. Their collective experiences of sacrifice and survival have shaped their values and worldviews, emphasizing hard work, loyalty, and perseverance[1].

In contrast, the baby boomers grew up during a period of unprecedented economic prosperity and social change. The post-war boom, the civil rights movement, and the counterculture revolution of the 1960s influenced their ideals of freedom, equality, and self-expression. This generation witnessed the moon landing, the rise of rock and roll, and the fight for civil rights, all of which left an indelible mark on their collective consciousness[2].

Generation X, often called the "latchkey" generation, experienced the rise of dual-income households and higher divorce rates, which fostered independence and self-reliance[3]. This generation grew up during the advent of personal computers and the early stages of globalization, shaping their adaptability and pragmatic approach to life[4].

Millennials, on the other hand, came of age during the digital revolution and the Great Recession. Their formative years were marked by rapid technological advancements, economic uncertainty, and a shifting job market. As a result, they value connectivity, inclusivity, and purpose-driven work[5]. This generation is characterized by their fluency in digital communication and their desire for meaningful, impactful careers[6].

Generation Z, the true digital natives, have never known a world without the internet. Their upbringing in an era of smartphones, social media, and instant access to information has profoundly influenced their communication styles, identities, and worldviews[7]. This generation is highly aware of global issues, deeply engaged in social activism, and adept at navigating the complexities of the digital age[8].

Learning from the Past

Understanding the historical contexts that shape each generation allows us to appreciate their unique strengths and challenges. By learning from the past, we can avoid repeating mistakes and build on the successes of those who came before us. This historical awareness fosters a sense of continuity and connection, reminding us that we are part of a larger narrative that extends beyond our individual lifetimes.

One of the most valuable lessons we can learn from the past is the importance of resilience. The silent generation's experiences of hardship and recovery during the Great Depression and World War II demonstrate the human capacity for endurance and renewal[9]. Their stories of overcoming adversity can inspire younger generations to persevere in the face of modern challenges, whether economic, social, or environmental.

Similarly, the social movements of the baby boomers offer powerful examples of collective action and the fight for justice. The civil rights movement, the women's liberation movement, and the anti-war protests of the 1960s and 1970s highlight the potential for positive change when people come together to challenge injustice and demand equality[10]. These historical moments serve as a reminder that progress is possible, even in the face of significant obstacles.

The entrepreneurial spirit and technological innovation of Generation X have also left a lasting legacy. As pioneers of the digital age, they have shown how adaptability and a willingness to embrace change can lead to groundbreaking advancements and new opportunities[11]. Their journey from analog to digital serves as a testament to the power of innovation and the importance of staying open to new possibilities.

Bridging Generational Gaps

Recognizing the power of the past helps us bridge generational gaps by fostering mutual respect and understanding. When we acknowledge the historical contexts that shape each generation's values and perspectives, we can move beyond stereotypes and misconceptions. Instead of viewing other generations through a lens of judgment, we can approach them with curiosity and empathy.

Intergenerational dialogue is a crucial tool in this process. By creating spaces where different generations can share their stories and experiences, we can build bridges of understanding and appreciation. Storytelling, in particular, is a powerful way to connect across generations. When we listen to the narratives of those who came before us, we gain insight into their struggles, triumphs, and lessons learned[12].

Mentorship is another effective way to bridge generational divides. By pairing individuals from different generations, we can facilitate the exchange of knowledge, skills, and perspectives.

Older generations can offer valuable wisdom and experience, while younger generations can provide fresh ideas and technological expertise. This reciprocal relationship benefits both parties and strengthens the fabric of our communities[13].

Embracing the Legacy

As we move forward, it is essential to embrace the legacy of the past while also forging our own path. Each generation has a unique contribution to make, and by working together, we can create a more inclusive and prosperous future. The power of the past lies not only in its lessons but also in its ability to inspire us to strive for better.

By honoring the experiences and achievements of previous generations, we can build a foundation of respect and collaboration. This foundation enables us to tackle contemporary challenges with a sense of shared purpose and collective strength. Whether addressing climate change, economic inequality, or social justice, the combined efforts of all generations are needed to create lasting solutions.

In conclusion, the power of the past is a vital force in our journey to unite generations. By understanding the historical contexts that shape our identities and values, we can foster empathy and mutual respect. Through intergenerational dialogue, mentorship, and collaboration, we can bridge generational gaps and create a society where the strengths of each generation are recognized and celebrated. As we embrace the legacy of the past, we pave the way for a future of mutual growth, success, and prosperity.

Exercise: Bridging Generational Gaps

Objective:

To foster understanding, empathy, and collaboration between different generations by exploring personal experiences, values, and perspectives.

Instructions:

1. Identify Participants:

- Select at least three individuals from different generations (e.g., Silent Generation, Baby Boomers, Generation X, Millennials, Generation Z). This can be done within a family, workplace, or community setting.

2. Preparation:

- Provide each participant with a brief overview of the historical contexts and defining events of their generation. Use summaries from the chapter for reference.
- Ask participants to prepare a short story (2-3 minutes) about a significant experience or event that shaped their values and perspectives.

3. Group Discussion:

- Gather participants in a comfortable, inclusive setting.

- Each participant takes turns sharing their story with the group. Encourage active listening, with no interruptions or judgments.
- After each story, allow for a brief Q&A session where other participants can ask questions to gain a deeper understanding of the storyteller's experience.

4. Reflective Exercise:

- After all stories have been shared, provide participants with reflection sheets containing the following prompts:
- ✓ What common themes did you notice among the different stories?
- ✓ How did each story contribute to your understanding of that generation's values and perspectives?
- ✓ What stereotypes or misconceptions did you have about other generations that were challenged by these stories?
- ✓ How can you apply the lessons learned from these stories in your own life or work?

5. Action Plan:

- Divide participants into small intergenerational groups.
- Each group should brainstorm and list practical ways to bridge generational gaps in their respective environments (e.g., workplace, community, family). Focus on fostering respect, collaboration, and mutual support.

- Groups share their action plans with the entire group, discussing how they can implement these strategies and what benefits they expect to see.

6. Follow-Up:

- Schedule a follow-up meeting (e.g., after one month) to discuss the progress and challenges faced while implementing the action plans.
- Encourage participants to share success stories and provide feedback on what worked well and what could be improved.

Expected Outcomes:

- Enhanced understanding and empathy between generations.
- Reduced stereotypes and misconceptions.
- Practical strategies for fostering intergenerational collaboration and respect.
- Strengthened relationships and improved communication across generational lines.

Evaluation:

- Participants complete a feedback form rating their experience and the effectiveness of the exercise.
- Measure success by tracking improvements in intergenerational interactions, such as increased

collaboration, reduced conflicts, and positive feedback from participants.

By engaging in this exercise, readers will not only deepen their understanding of the concepts discussed in the chapter but also gain practical skills to implement in their daily lives, contributing to a more harmonious and connected society.

NOTES:

Chapter 2: Bridging the Gap

The generational divide often seems like a chasm, filled with misunderstandings and differing perspectives. However, bridging this gap is not only possible but essential for fostering mutual growth, success, and prosperity. To achieve this, we must approach intergenerational relationships with openness, respect, and a genuine desire to understand one another. This chapter delves into practical strategies and insights for overcoming generational differences and building stronger, more cohesive communities.

Understanding Generational Differences

Before we can bridge the gap, we need to understand what creates it. Each generation has been shaped by the unique socio-economic, technological, and cultural conditions of its time. These influences have resulted in distinct values, behaviors, and communication styles. By recognizing these differences, we can begin to appreciate the diverse perspectives each generation brings to the table.

Silent Generation and Baby Boomers

The Silent Generation and Baby Boomers grew up in eras of significant economic and social change. The Silent Generation, having lived through the Great Depression and World War II, values hard work, resilience, and loyalty. They tend to have a strong sense of duty and community[1].

Baby Boomers, born during a period of post-war prosperity, experienced the civil rights movement, the Vietnam War, and the sexual revolution. They value personal freedom, social justice, and self-expression. These experiences have shaped their optimistic outlook and their belief in the possibility of change through collective action[2].

Generation X

Generation X, often referred to as the "latchkey generation," grew up during a time of increasing divorce rates and dual-income households. They are known for their independence, adaptability, and pragmatism. Having witnessed the transition from an industrial to a digital economy, they are comfortable with change and often act as a bridge between older and younger generations[3].

Millennials

Millennials came of age during the digital revolution and the Great Recession. They are characterized by their fluency in technology, a strong sense of social responsibility, and a desire for meaningful work. Connectivity and inclusivity are central to their values, and they often seek out collaborative and purpose-driven environments[4].

Generation Z

Generation Z, the true digital natives, have grown up with the internet and social media as integral parts of their lives. They are highly adept at navigating the digital world and are deeply engaged in social and environmental issues. This generation values authenticity, diversity, and direct communication[5].

Strategies for Bridging the Gap

To bridge the generational gap, we must implement strategies that foster understanding, respect, and collaboration. Here are some practical approaches:

1. Promote Open Communication

Effective communication is the cornerstone of any successful relationship. Encourage open and honest dialogue between generations. Create spaces where individuals feel safe to share their experiences, values, and perspectives without fear of judgment. Listening actively and empathetically is crucial. When people feel heard and understood, they are more likely to reciprocate with respect and openness[6].

2. Foster Intergenerational Collaboration

Workplaces, communities, and families can benefit greatly from intergenerational collaboration. Diverse teams bring together a wide range of skills, experiences, and viewpoints, leading to more innovative solutions and better decision-making. Encourage projects that require collaboration between different age groups and ensure that each generation's contributions are valued and recognized[7].

3. Implement Mentorship Programs

Mentorship is a powerful tool for bridging generational gaps. Establish mentorship programs that pair individuals from different generations. This allows for the exchange of knowledge, skills, and perspectives. Older generations can offer valuable insights and experience, while younger generations can provide fresh ideas and technological expertise. Mentorship fosters mutual respect and helps build strong, supportive relationships[8].

4. Encourage Lifelong Learning

Promote a culture of lifelong learning where individuals of all ages are encouraged to continuously develop their skills and knowledge. Offer training and development opportunities that cater to different generations, ensuring that everyone has access to the resources they need to succeed. This not only helps individuals stay relevant in a rapidly changing world but also fosters a sense of shared purpose and growth[9].

5. Celebrate Diversity and Inclusion

Acknowledge and celebrate the diversity of experiences, values, and perspectives that each generation brings. Create inclusive environments where everyone feels valued and respected. This can be achieved through policies, practices, and initiatives that promote diversity and inclusion. Celebrating milestones and achievements of different generations can also help build a sense of community and shared identity[10].

Overcoming Challenges

While the benefits of bridging generational gaps are clear, there are challenges to be aware of. Stereotypes and biases can hinder understanding and cooperation. It's important to address these issues head-on by fostering a culture of openness and respect. Encourage individuals to challenge their own assumptions and be willing to learn from others[11].

Resistance to change can also be a barrier. Some individuals may be hesitant to adopt new ways of thinking or working. To overcome this, provide support and encouragement, and highlight the benefits of intergenerational collaboration. Change is a gradual process, and patience and persistence are key[12].

The Role of Leadership

Leadership plays a crucial role in bridging generational gaps. Leaders set the tone for the organization or community and can influence attitudes and behaviors. By modeling inclusive and respectful behavior, leaders can inspire others to follow suit. Encourage leaders to actively engage with individuals from different generations, seek out their input, and champion initiatives that promote intergenerational understanding and collaboration[13].

Case Studies

To illustrate the effectiveness of these strategies, consider the following case studies:

Case Study 1: Corporate Mentorship Program

A multinational corporation implemented a mentorship program pairing senior executives with young professionals. The program focused on knowledge exchange, leadership development, and fostering innovation. As a result, the company saw increased employee engagement, improved performance, and a more cohesive organizational culture[14].

Case Study 2: Community Intergenerational Project

A community organization launched an intergenerational project where older adults and teenagers collaborated on a local history project. The initiative not only preserved valuable historical knowledge but also built strong relationships between participants. The project enhanced community cohesion and provided a platform for mutual learning and respect[15].

Bridging the generational gap is not only possible but essential for creating a harmonious and prosperous society. By understanding the unique experiences and values of each generation, promoting open communication, fostering collaboration, and implementing supportive programs, we can overcome differences and build stronger, more cohesive communities. Leadership, patience, and a commitment to inclusivity are key to this process. Together, we can bridge the generational divide and pave the way for mutual growth, success, and prosperity.

Exercise: Building Bridges Across Generations

Objective:

To enhance understanding, empathy, and collaboration between different generations by actively engaging in discussions, reflections, and collaborative projects.

Instructions:

1. Select Participants:

- Gather a diverse group of individuals representing at least three different generations (e.g., Silent Generation, Baby Boomers, Generation X, Millennials, Generation Z). This can be done within a workplace, community organization, or family setting.

2. Icebreaker Activity:

- Begin with a simple icebreaker activity to help participants get to know each other. For example, ask each person to share their name, generation, and a fun fact or hobby they enjoy.

3. Story Sharing Session:

- Provide each participant with a few minutes to share a personal story that highlights a significant experience or event that shaped their values and perspectives. Encourage active listening, ensuring that each speaker is given full attention without interruptions.

- After each story, allow a brief period for questions and reflections from other participants to foster understanding and empathy.

4. Reflection Exercise:

- Distribute reflection sheets to participants with the following prompts:
- ✓ Identify at least one value or perspective from each generation that resonates with you.
- ✓ Reflect on a stereotype or misconception you had about another generation that was challenged during the story sharing.
- ✓ Write down any new insights or lessons learned from the stories shared.

5. Group Discussion:

- Facilitate a group discussion based on the reflections. Encourage participants to share their insights and how their understanding of other generations has evolved.
- Discuss common themes and values that emerged from the stories, highlighting similarities and differences.

6. Intergenerational Collaboration Project:

- Divide participants into small intergenerational teams and assign a collaborative project that addresses a community or organizational challenge. Examples include:
- ✓ Planning a community event that promotes cultural heritage and inclusivity.
- ✓ Developing a proposal for a workplace initiative that fosters employee well-being.
- ✓ Creating a social media campaign that addresses a pressing social issue.

- Ensure that each team member has a defined role and that all voices are heard during the planning and execution stages.

7. Presentation and Feedback:

- Have each team present their project to the larger group. Encourage creative presentations, such as using visuals, storytelling, or role-playing.
- Provide constructive feedback, focusing on the strengths of the project and areas for improvement.
- Celebrate the efforts and achievements of each team, emphasizing the value of intergenerational collaboration.

8. Action Plan:

- Ask each participant to create a personal action plan based on the exercise. This plan should include:
- ✓ Specific steps they will take to foster intergenerational understanding and collaboration in their daily lives.
- ✓ Goals for engaging with individuals from different generations in meaningful ways.
- ✓ Strategies for applying the lessons learned from the exercise to their personal or professional environments.

9. Follow-Up Session:

- Schedule a follow-up session a few weeks later to discuss progress and challenges. Encourage participants to share their experiences and any changes they have noticed in their interactions with other generations.

- Provide additional support and resources as needed to help participants continue building bridges across generations.

Expected Outcomes:

- Enhanced understanding and empathy between generations.
- Reduced stereotypes and misconceptions.
- Practical experience in intergenerational collaboration.
- Strengthened relationships and improved communication across generational lines.
- Personal commitment to fostering intergenerational harmony in everyday life.

Evaluation:

- Participants complete a feedback form rating their experience and the effectiveness of the exercise.
- Measure success by tracking improvements in intergenerational interactions, such as increased collaboration, reduced conflicts, and positive feedback from participants.

- By engaging in this exercise, readers will deepen their understanding of the concepts discussed in the chapter and gain practical skills to implement in their daily lives, contributing to a more harmonious and connected society.

Chapter 3: The Digital Natives

In an era defined by rapid technological advancement, Generation Z stands at the forefront as the true digital natives. Born from 1997 onwards, this generation has never known a world without the internet, smartphones, and social media. Their lives are deeply intertwined with technology, shaping their experiences, communication styles, and worldview in profound ways. Understanding Generation Z, or the digital natives, is essential for bridging generational gaps and fostering intergenerational collaboration. This chapter explores the defining characteristics of digital natives, their impact on society, and strategies for engaging with and learning from this technologically adept generation.

Defining Characteristics of Digital Natives

Digital natives are unique in many ways, marked by their inherent familiarity with digital technology. This familiarity is not merely about using gadgets but encompasses a broader set of skills and behaviors that distinguish them from previous generations.

1. **Technological Fluency**: Digital natives are highly proficient with technology. From an early age, they have been exposed to a wide array of digital devices and platforms, making them adept at navigating the digital landscape. This fluency allows them to quickly learn and

adapt to new technologies, making them invaluable in today's tech-driven world[1].

2. **Multitasking Abilities**: Growing up in a hyper-connected environment has endowed digital natives with the ability to multitask effectively. They can seamlessly switch between different tasks and digital platforms, managing various streams of information simultaneously[2]. While this can lead to concerns about attention span, it also highlights their capacity to handle complex, multi-faceted situations.

3. **Global Awareness**: The internet has made the world smaller, and digital natives have a heightened awareness of global issues. Social media and online platforms provide them with instant access to news and events from around the world, fostering a sense of global citizenship[3]. This global perspective often drives their engagement in social and environmental activism.

4. **Value of Authenticity**: Authenticity is a core value for digital natives. They are drawn to brands, influencers, and leaders who are genuine and transparent. This preference for authenticity influences their interactions and the way they present themselves online[4].

5. **Social Connectivity**: Digital natives are highly connected through social media. These platforms serve as their primary means of communication, socialization,

and self-expression. They use social media not only to stay in touch with friends and family but also to build communities around shared interests and causes[5].

Impact of Digital Natives on Society

The influence of digital natives extends beyond their personal characteristics to shape various aspects of society. Their behaviors and preferences are driving significant changes in technology, education, work, and social norms.

1. **Technology and Innovation**: Digital natives are at the forefront of technological innovation. Their demand for cutting-edge technology drives the development of new gadgets, applications, and digital solutions. Companies are constantly evolving to meet the expectations of this tech-savvy generation[6].

2. **Education**: The educational landscape is being transformed by the presence of digital natives. Traditional teaching methods are being supplemented or replaced by digital tools and platforms that cater to their learning styles. Online courses, interactive content, and educational apps are becoming integral parts of the learning experience[7].

3. **Workplace Dynamics**: As digital natives enter the workforce, they are redefining workplace dynamics. They value flexibility, remote work options, and collaborative environments. Organizations are adapting to these

preferences by implementing digital tools that facilitate remote work and creating spaces that encourage teamwork and innovation[8].

4. **Social Change and Activism**: Digital natives are using their connectivity and global awareness to drive social change. They leverage social media to raise awareness, mobilize support, and advocate for various causes, from climate change to social justice. Their activism is often characterized by a sense of urgency and a desire for immediate impact[9].

Strategies for Engaging with Digital Natives

To effectively engage with digital natives, it is crucial to understand their values, preferences, and communication styles. Here are some strategies to build meaningful connections with this generation:

1. **Embrace Technology**: Utilize digital tools and platforms to communicate and collaborate with digital natives. Be open to adopting new technologies that enhance interaction and engagement. Whether in the workplace, educational settings, or social environments, leveraging technology can bridge gaps and foster collaboration[10].

2. **Foster Authenticity**: Be genuine and transparent in your interactions. Digital natives value authenticity and can quickly discern insincerity. Whether in personal

relationships, marketing, or leadership, showing authenticity can build trust and respect[11].

3. **Promote Flexibility**: Offer flexibility in how and where tasks are completed. Digital natives appreciate environments that allow them to balance work, learning, and personal life effectively. Flexible work arrangements and adaptive learning environments can enhance their productivity and satisfaction[12].

4. **Encourage Social Responsibility**: Engage digital natives in social and environmental initiatives. Their strong sense of global citizenship and desire to make a difference can be harnessed to drive positive change. Provide opportunities for them to participate in meaningful projects and causes[13].

5. **Create Collaborative Spaces**: Design spaces that encourage collaboration and creativity. Digital natives thrive in environments that support teamwork and the exchange of ideas. Whether physical or virtual, creating collaborative spaces can enhance their engagement and innovation[14].

Understanding and engaging with digital natives is essential for building a cohesive and prosperous society. Their technological fluency, multitasking abilities, global awareness, and value for authenticity are reshaping various aspects of our world. By embracing technology, fostering authenticity, promoting flexibility, encouraging social responsibility, and creating collaborative spaces, we can bridge generational gaps and harness the strengths of this dynamic generation.

The digital natives are not just the future; they are shaping the present. By recognizing and valuing their contributions, we can learn from them and work together to create a better, more connected world. As we continue our journey of bridging generational gaps, let us embrace the insights and innovations that digital natives bring to the table, fostering a culture of mutual respect, understanding, and collaboration.

Exercise: Engaging with Digital Natives

Objective:

To enhance understanding, empathy, and collaboration with digital natives by engaging in interactive activities and reflections.

Instructions:

1. Participant Selection:

- Form a group with participants from at least three different generations, including Generation Z. This can be done within a workplace, educational institution, or community group.

2. Introduction Session:

- Begin with a brief introduction about the purpose of the exercise and the importance of understanding and engaging with digital natives.

3. Technology Showcase:

- Ask the digital natives (Generation Z participants) to showcase their favorite digital tools, apps, or platforms. Each participant should explain why they like it, how they use it, and how it benefits their daily life or work.

4. Collaborative Digital Project:

- Divide participants into intergenerational teams. Each team will work on a collaborative digital project. Examples include:
- ✓ Creating a short video on a social issue using a popular video-editing app.
- ✓ Designing a social media campaign for a community event.
- ✓ Developing a simple website or blog on a shared interest.

5. Reflection Session:

- After completing the projects, bring all participants together for a reflection session. Use the following prompts:
- ✓ What did you learn about digital tools and platforms from the digital natives?

✓ How did the collaboration process differ from your usual experiences?

✓ What challenges did you encounter, and how did you overcome them?

✓ How can you apply these digital tools and skills in your own work or daily life?

6. Open Dialogue:

- Facilitate an open dialogue where participants from all generations share their perspectives on the digital tools used and the collaborative process. Encourage digital natives to provide tips and insights on effective technology use.

7. Action Plan:

- Ask each participant to create a personal action plan based on the exercise. This plan should include:
✓ Specific digital tools or skills they want to learn or improve.

✓ Steps they will take to engage more effectively with digital natives.

✓ Goals for integrating digital tools into their work or personal projects.

8.   **Follow-Up Session:**

- Schedule a follow-up session a month later to discuss progress and challenges. Encourage participants to share their successes, insights, and any further questions they have about engaging with digital technology and digital natives.

Expected Outcomes:

- Enhanced understanding and empathy between generations.
- Improved digital literacy and skills across all generations.
- Practical experience in using digital tools and platforms.
- Strengthened relationships and improved communication between generations.
- Personal commitment to ongoing learning and engagement with digital technology.

Evaluation:

- Participants complete a feedback form rating their experience and the effectiveness of the exercise.
- Measure success by tracking improvements in digital literacy, increased collaboration, and positive feedback from participants.

By engaging in this exercise, readers will not only deepen their understanding of digital natives and their impact on society but also gain practical skills and strategies for effective intergenerational collaboration and digital engagement.

Chapter 4: Collaborative Success

In today's interconnected world, the concept of success is increasingly seen as a collaborative effort rather than an individual achievement. This shift is driven by the realization that diverse perspectives, skills, and experiences can significantly enhance problem-solving and innovation. For generations to truly unite and achieve mutual growth, success, and prosperity, we must embrace collaboration. This chapter explores the essence of collaborative success, the benefits it brings, and practical strategies for fostering effective collaboration across generations.

The Essence of Collaborative Success

Collaborative success is the product of collective effort, where individuals work together towards a common goal. It is characterized by shared responsibility, mutual respect, and open communication. In a collaborative environment, each participant's contributions are valued, and diverse viewpoints are leveraged to create more comprehensive and effective solutions[1].

One of the key aspects of collaborative success is the recognition that no single person has all the answers. By pooling knowledge and resources, we can overcome complex challenges and drive innovation. Collaboration allows us to combine the strengths of different generations, creating a synergy that leads to greater achievements than what any one generation could accomplish alone[2].

Benefits of Collaborative Success

1. **Enhanced Creativity and Innovation**: When people from different backgrounds and generations collaborate, they bring unique ideas and perspectives to the table. This diversity fuels creativity and innovation, leading to the development of novel solutions and approaches[3].

2. **Improved Problem-Solving**: Collaborative efforts often result in more effective problem-solving. Diverse teams can approach problems from various angles, considering a wider range of factors and potential solutions. This comprehensive approach reduces blind spots and increases the likelihood of finding effective solutions[4].

3. **Increased Engagement and Motivation**: Collaboration fosters a sense of ownership and belonging among team members. When individuals feel that their contributions are valued and that they are part of something larger than themselves, their engagement and motivation levels rise[5].

4. **Strengthened Relationships**: Working together towards a common goal helps build trust and strengthen relationships. These strong relationships are essential for creating cohesive teams and communities that can support each other in achieving long-term success[6].

5. **Mutual Learning and Growth**: Collaborative success provides opportunities for mutual learning and growth. Different generations can share their knowledge and experiences, enriching each other's understanding and capabilities. This continuous exchange of ideas promotes personal and professional development[7].

Strategies for Fostering Collaborative Success

To achieve collaborative success, it is crucial to create an environment that encourages and supports collaboration. Here are some practical strategies to foster effective collaboration across generations:

1. **Promote Open Communication**: Open and transparent communication is the foundation of successful collaboration. Encourage team members to share their ideas, concerns, and feedback openly. Create a culture where all voices are heard and valued, regardless of age or experience[8].

2. **Leverage Technology**: Utilize digital tools and platforms to facilitate collaboration. Technology can bridge geographical and generational gaps, making it easier for teams to work together regardless of location. Use collaboration software, video conferencing, and project management tools to streamline communication and coordination[9].

3. **Create Inclusive Environments**: Foster an inclusive culture where diversity is celebrated and all team members feel respected and valued. This includes being mindful of generational differences and finding ways to integrate diverse perspectives into the collaborative process[10].

4. **Establish Clear Goals and Roles**: Clearly define the goals of the collaborative effort and the roles of each team member. This clarity helps prevent misunderstandings and ensures that everyone is aligned and working towards the same objectives. Assign roles based on individuals' strengths and expertise, making sure to leverage the unique skills of each generation[11].

5. **Encourage Flexibility and Adaptability**: Collaboration often requires flexibility and adaptability. Be open to new ideas and approaches and encourage team members to experiment and take calculated risks. This willingness to adapt fosters a dynamic and innovative collaborative environment[12].

6. **Provide Training and Support**: Equip team members with the skills and knowledge they need to collaborate effectively. Offer training on communication, teamwork, and conflict resolution. Provide ongoing support and resources to help teams navigate challenges and maintain productive collaboration[13].

7. **Celebrate Successes**: Recognize and celebrate collaborative successes, both big and small. Celebrating achievements reinforces the value of collaboration and motivates team members to continue working together. Acknowledging contributions from all generations fosters a sense of shared accomplishment and pride[14].

Case Studies of Collaborative Success

Case Study 1: Cross-Generational Innovation in Healthcare

A healthcare organization faced the challenge of improving patient care while reducing costs. They formed a cross-generational team that included seasoned doctors, young medical professionals, and tech-savvy millennials. By combining their diverse expertise, the team developed an innovative telemedicine program that enhanced patient access to care and significantly reduced costs. The success of this collaborative effort was driven by open communication, mutual respect, and the integration of diverse perspectives[15].

Case Study 2: Community Revitalization Project

In a small town struggling with economic decline, a community revitalization project brought together residents from different generations. Older residents contributed their historical knowledge and experience, while younger generations provided fresh ideas and energy. Through collaborative efforts, they revitalized the town's main street, attracting new businesses and fostering a sense of community pride. The project's success highlighted the power of intergenerational collaboration in achieving common goals[16].

Overcoming Challenges to Collaboration

While the benefits of collaborative success are clear, there are challenges that need to be addressed. These include:

- **Stereotypes and Biases**: Overcoming generational stereotypes and biases is essential for effective collaboration. Encourage team members to challenge their assumptions and focus on the strengths and contributions of each individual[17].

- **Communication Barriers**: Differences in communication styles can create misunderstandings. Provide training on effective communication and create opportunities for team members to learn about each other's preferred communication methods[18].

- **Resistance to Change**: Some individuals may be resistant to new ways of working. Address this resistance by highlighting the benefits of collaboration and providing support to help team members adapt to change[19].

Collaborative success is a powerful approach that harnesses the strengths of different generations to achieve common goals. By promoting open communication, leveraging technology, creating inclusive environments, and providing training and support, we can foster effective collaboration across generations. The benefits of collaborative success, including enhanced creativity, improved problem-solving, increased engagement, strengthened relationships, and mutual learning, make it a vital strategy for achieving mutual growth, success, and prosperity.

As we continue our journey of bridging generational gaps, let us embrace the power of collaboration and work together to build a better future. Through collaborative success, we can create a more connected, innovative, and resilient society where all generations thrive.

Exercise: Fostering Collaborative Success

Objective:

To enhance understanding and practical application of collaborative success by engaging participants in intergenerational teamwork, promoting mutual respect, and leveraging diverse perspectives.

Instructions:

1. Participant Selection:

- Form small groups consisting of individuals from different generations, including members from at least three different generations (e.g., Baby Boomers, Generation X, Millennials, Generation Z).

2. Introduction Session:

- Begin with a brief introduction explaining the importance of collaborative success and the objectives of the exercise.

3. Icebreaker Activity:

- Each participant shares a brief story about a successful collaboration experience or a challenge they faced that could have benefited from better collaboration.

4. Identifying Common Goals:

- Ask each group to identify a common goal or challenge they would like to address. This could be a workplace issue, a community project, or a social problem.

5. Brainstorming Session:

- Use the following prompts to guide the brainstorming:
- ✓ What are the unique strengths and perspectives each generation brings to the table?
- ✓ How can the experiences of older generations inform the approach to this challenge?
- ✓ What innovative ideas can younger generations contribute to solving this problem?

6.Action Plan Development:

- Each group should develop a detailed action plan that integrates the strengths of different generations. The action plan should include:
- ✓ A clear definition of the goal or challenge.
- ✓ Specific objectives and milestones.
- ✓ Roles and responsibilities for each team member.
- ✓ Steps to implement the plan, leveraging both traditional wisdom and modern innovation.
- ✓ Potential challenges and strategies to overcome them.

7. Utilizing Technology:

Encourage groups to use digital tools and platforms to facilitate collaboration. This includes collaboration software, video conferencing tools, and project management apps.

8. Presentation and Feedback:

- Have each group present their action plan to the larger group. Encourage creative presentations that highlight the integration of diverse perspectives.
- Facilitate a feedback session where other participants can ask questions, provide constructive feedback, and suggest additional ideas.

9. Implementation Strategy:

- Encourage participants to take their action plans back to their workplaces or communities and implement them.
- Schedule a follow-up session (e.g., after one month) where participants can share their experiences, successes, and challenges faced during implementation.
- Discuss any adjustments or improvements made to the action plans based on real-world feedback.

10. Reflection and Learning:

- Conclude with a reflection session where participants discuss the key lessons learned from the exercise.
- Use the following prompts:
- What new insights did you gain about the value of collaboration?
- How did the collaboration between different generations enhance the problem-solving process?
- What skills or knowledge did you acquire from this exercise that you can apply in your future work or personal life?

Expected Outcomes:

- Enhanced understanding of the benefits and strategies of collaborative success.
- Practical experience in integrating diverse perspectives to solve real-world problems.

- Strengthened intergenerational relationships and improved communication.
- Development of actionable plans that participants can implement in their own contexts.
- Increased motivation to leverage the strengths of different generations for mutual growth and success.

Evaluation:

- Participants complete a feedback form rating their experience and the effectiveness of the exercise.
- Measure success by tracking the implementation of action plans and gathering feedback on the outcomes.
- Conduct follow-up sessions to assess long-term impact and sustainability of the collaborative approaches.

By engaging in this exercise, readers will deepen their understanding of the concepts discussed in the chapter and gain practical skills for fostering collaborative success in their personal and professional lives.

Chapter 5: Wisdom Meets Innovation

In the landscape of modern society, the meeting of wisdom and innovation presents a powerful opportunity for growth and transformation. Wisdom, derived from years of experience and deep understanding, and innovation, driven by fresh ideas and new technologies, can together create a dynamic synergy. This chapter explores how different generations can leverage their unique strengths to foster mutual growth, success, and prosperity.

The Value of Wisdom

Wisdom is a treasure trove of knowledge, insights, and lessons learned over time. It encompasses not only factual knowledge but also the ability to apply that knowledge judiciously. Individuals from older generations, such as the Silent Generation and Baby Boomers, bring a wealth of experience that can guide and inform younger generations.

1. **Historical Perspective**: Older generations have witnessed significant historical events and societal changes. Their firsthand experiences provide valuable context and understanding of how past decisions and actions have shaped the present[1]. This perspective can help younger generations avoid repeating mistakes and build on past successes.

2. **Emotional Intelligence**: With age often comes greater emotional intelligence—the ability to recognize, understand, and manage one's own emotions and those of others[2]. This skill is crucial for effective leadership, conflict resolution, and building strong, collaborative relationships.

3. **Resilience**: Having navigated various challenges and adversities, older generations often possess a high degree of resilience[3]. Their stories of overcoming difficulties can inspire and motivate younger individuals, teaching them the value of perseverance and adaptability.

The Power of Innovation

Innovation, on the other hand, is the engine of progress. It involves the creation and implementation of new ideas, processes, and technologies that drive change and improvement. Younger generations, particularly Millennials and Generation Z, are at the forefront of this innovative wave.

1. **Technological Proficiency**: Digital natives, especially Generation Z, have grown up with technology as an integral part of their lives[4]. Their fluency with digital tools and platforms allows them to quickly adapt to new technologies and leverage them to solve problems and create new opportunities.

2. **Creative Problem-Solving**: Younger generations tend to approach problems with a fresh perspective, unencumbered by traditional ways of thinking[5]. This creativity can lead to innovative solutions that might not be apparent to those with a more conventional mindset.

3. **Social Connectivity**: The younger generations are highly connected through social media and other digital platforms[6]. This connectivity not only facilitates the rapid exchange of ideas but also enables the mobilization of collective action towards common goals.

Bridging the Generational Divide

To harness the full potential of wisdom and innovation, it is essential to bridge the generational divide and create opportunities for meaningful collaboration. Here are some strategies to achieve this:

1. **Foster Intergenerational Dialogue**: Create spaces for open and respectful dialogue between generations. Encourage older individuals to share their experiences and insights, while also listening to and valuing the fresh perspectives of younger generations[7].

2. **Mentorship Programs**: Establish mentorship programs that pair experienced professionals with younger individuals. This two-way exchange allows mentors to impart wisdom and guidance, while mentees can share new ideas and technological skills[8].

3. **Collaborative Projects**: Promote projects that require intergenerational collaboration. By working together on common goals, individuals from different generations can learn from each other and combine their strengths to achieve greater outcomes[9].

4. **Lifelong Learning**: Encourage a culture of lifelong learning where individuals of all ages are motivated to continually develop their skills and knowledge[10]. Offer training and development opportunities that cater to both seasoned professionals and those just starting their careers.

Case Studies of Successful Integration

Case Study 1: The Tech-Savvy Mentor

A large corporation implemented a reverse mentorship program where younger employees mentored senior executives on digital technologies and social media. This initiative not only improved the digital literacy of the leadership team but also fostered mutual respect and understanding between generations[11]. The younger mentors gained confidence and leadership skills, while the executives became more adept at leveraging technology to drive business success.

Case Study 2: Community Innovation Hub

In a small town, a community center launched an innovation hub that brought together retirees and young entrepreneurs. The retirees shared their business acumen and life experiences, while the entrepreneurs introduced cutting-edge technologies and innovative business models[12]. This collaboration led to the development of several successful startups and revitalized the local economy.

Overcoming Challenges

While the integration of wisdom and innovation offers significant benefits, it also comes with challenges. These include:

- **Stereotypes and Biases**: Overcoming stereotypes and biases about different generations is crucial for effective collaboration. Encourage individuals to challenge their assumptions and appreciate the unique strengths of each generation[13].

- **Communication Barriers**: Different communication styles can lead to misunderstandings. Provide training on effective communication and create opportunities for team members to learn about each other's preferred communication methods[14].

- **Resistance to Change**: Some individuals may be resistant to new ways of thinking or working. Address this resistance by highlighting the benefits of intergenerational collaboration and providing support to help individuals adapt to change[15].

The intersection of wisdom and innovation holds immense potential for driving progress and achieving mutual growth, success, and prosperity. By fostering intergenerational collaboration, we can leverage the rich experiences of older generations and the innovative spirit of younger ones to create a more dynamic and resilient society.

As we move forward, let us embrace the wisdom of the past while eagerly exploring the innovations of the future. Together, we can build a world where each generation's strengths are recognized and valued, and where collaborative efforts lead to extraordinary achievements.

In this journey, remember that every generation has something valuable to offer. By bridging the generational divide and fostering a culture of mutual respect and learning, we can unlock the full potential of wisdom and innovation. This approach not only enriches our lives but also paves the way for a brighter, more prosperous future for all.

Exercise: Integrating Wisdom and Innovation

Objective:

To facilitate the integration of wisdom and innovation through intergenerational collaboration, enhancing participants' understanding and application of these concepts in real-world scenarios.

Instructions:

1. Participant Selection:
- Form small groups consisting of individuals from different generations, including at least one member from the Silent Generation/Baby Boomers, Generation X, Millennials, and Generation Z.

2. Introduction Session:
- Begin with a brief introduction explaining the importance of integrating wisdom and innovation and the objectives of the exercise.

3. Icebreaker Activity:
- Have each participant share a brief story about a significant learning experience in their life (for older participants) or an innovative idea they are passionate about (for younger participants).

4. Brainstorming Session:

- Ask each group to identify a real-world challenge that could benefit from both wisdom and innovation. This could be a workplace issue, community project, or social problem.
- Use the following prompts to guide the brainstorming:
- ✓ How can the experience and knowledge of older generations contribute to solving this problem?
- ✓ What innovative approaches or technologies can younger generations bring to the table?

5. Action Plan Development:

- Each group should develop a detailed action plan that combines the wisdom and insights from older generations with the innovative ideas and skills of younger generations.
- The action plan should include:
- ✓ A clear definition of the problem.
- ✓ Objectives and goals for addressing the problem.
- ✓ Specific roles and contributions of each generation.
- ✓ Steps to implement the plan, leveraging both traditional wisdom and modern innovation.
- ✓ Potential challenges and strategies to overcome them.

6. Presentation and Feedback:

- Have each group present their action plan to the larger group. Encourage creative presentations that highlight the integration of wisdom and innovation.
- After each presentation, facilitate a feedback session where other participants can ask questions, provide constructive feedback, and suggest additional ideas.

7. Implementation Strategy:

- Encourage participants to take their action plans back to their workplaces or communities and implement them.
- Provide a follow-up session (e.g., after one month) where participants can share their experiences, successes, and challenges faced during implementation.
- Discuss any adjustments or improvements made to the action plans based on real-world feedback.

8. Reflection and Learning:

- Conclude with a reflection session where participants discuss the key lessons learned from the exercise.
- Use the following prompts:
- ✓ What new insights did you gain about the value of integrating wisdom and innovation?
- ✓ How did the collaboration between different generations enhance the problem-solving process?

✓ What skills or knowledge did you acquire from this exercise that you can apply in your future work or personal life?

Expected Outcomes:

- Enhanced understanding of the complementary roles of wisdom and innovation.
- Practical experience in integrating diverse perspectives and skills to solve real-world problems.
- Strengthened intergenerational relationships and improved communication.
- Development of actionable plans that participants can implement in their own contexts.
- Increased motivation to leverage the strengths of different generations for mutual growth and success.

Evaluation:

- Participants complete a feedback form rating their experience and the effectiveness of the exercise.
- Measure success by tracking the implementation of action plans and gathering feedback on the outcomes.
- Conduct follow-up sessions to assess long-term impact and sustainability of the integrated approaches.

By engaging in this exercise, readers will deepen their understanding of the concepts discussed in the chapter and gain practical skills for integrating wisdom and innovation in their personal and professional lives.

NOTES:

Chapter 6: Cultural and Social Synergy

In the mosaic of human society, each generation contributes its own unique cultural and social patterns, creating a rich tapestry that reflects our collective history, experiences, and aspirations. The concept of cultural and social synergy emerges from the understanding that these generational differences, rather than being divisive, can be harmonized to foster mutual growth, success, and prosperity. As we delve into this chapter, we will explore how bridging cultural and social gaps between generations can lead to a more inclusive, dynamic, and resilient society.

Understanding Cultural Diversity Across Generations

Cultural diversity is one of the most significant factors that define generational identities. Each generation grows up with its own set of cultural norms, values, and traditions, influenced by the socio-political and economic contexts of their formative years. For instance, Baby Boomers were shaped by the post-war era, marked by economic prosperity and social movements, whereas Millennials and Generation Z are digital natives, heavily influenced by technology and globalization[1,2].

Recognizing and appreciating these differences is the first step towards creating cultural and social synergy. When we understand where each generation is coming from, we can better appreciate their perspectives and contributions. This understanding fosters respect and opens up avenues for meaningful dialogue and collaboration[3].

The Role of Technology in Bridging Cultural Gaps

Technology plays a pivotal role in bridging generational cultural gaps. Social media platforms, for example, allow for the sharing of diverse cultural expressions across generations, creating opportunities for younger and older generations to engage with each other's cultural narratives. Online communities and forums provide spaces where people from different age groups can discuss common interests and concerns, leading to a greater understanding and appreciation of each other's cultural backgrounds[4].

Moreover, technology can be a tool for preserving and transmitting cultural heritage. Digital archives, virtual museums, and online educational resources make it possible for younger generations to access and learn about the cultural practices and traditions of their elders. This not only helps in preserving cultural heritage but also in fostering a sense of continuity and connection between generations[5].

Social Interactions and Generational Synergy

Social interactions are another crucial aspect of generational synergy. Intergenerational social interactions, whether in families, communities, or workplaces, can lead to a richer exchange of ideas and experiences. These interactions help in breaking down stereotypes and misconceptions that often create barriers between generations[6].

In family settings, activities such as storytelling, shared hobbies, and family traditions can strengthen the bond between generations. For instance, grandparents sharing stories from their youth can provide younger family members with valuable life lessons and a deeper understanding of their family history[7]. On the other hand, younger generations can introduce their elders to new technologies and contemporary cultural trends, creating a reciprocal learning environment[8].

In the workplace, intergenerational mentorship programs can be highly effective. Older employees can share their experience and expertise, while younger employees can bring fresh perspectives and innovative ideas. Such programs not only enhance individual growth but also contribute to a more dynamic and cohesive organizational culture[9].

Education as a Catalyst for Generational Integration

Education is a powerful catalyst for cultural and social synergy. Educational institutions have the potential to create environments where intergenerational learning and collaboration are encouraged. Intergenerational learning programs, where students and older adults learn together, can break down age-related barriers and foster mutual respect and understanding[10].

Curricula that include diverse cultural perspectives and histories help students appreciate the contributions of different generations. This inclusive approach to education ensures that the cultural and social knowledge of older generations is passed down, while also embracing the evolving cultural expressions of younger generations[11].

Creating Inclusive Communities

Communities that promote inclusivity and intergenerational engagement are better equipped to harness the benefits of cultural and social synergy. Community centers, clubs, and organizations can facilitate intergenerational activities and events that bring people of all ages together. These activities can range from cultural festivals and art exhibits to volunteer projects and recreational programs[12].

Inclusive communities also benefit from policies that support intergenerational interaction. For example, urban planning that includes shared public spaces, mixed-age housing, and accessible transportation can encourage social interaction across age groups. By designing communities that cater to the needs of all generations, we create environments where everyone can thrive[13].

The Economic and Social Benefits of Generational Synergy

The benefits of cultural and social synergy extend beyond personal and community growth; they have significant economic and social implications as well. Businesses that leverage the strengths of a diverse, multi-generational workforce are often more innovative and competitive. Diverse teams bring a wider range of perspectives and problem-solving approaches, leading to more creative solutions and better decision-making[14].

On a broader scale, societies that embrace intergenerational collaboration are more resilient and adaptable to change. The exchange of knowledge and skills between generations can drive social progress and economic development. Moreover, a society that values and respects its elders while empowering its youth creates a more harmonious and cohesive social fabric[15].

Moving Forward: Embracing Our Shared Cultural and Social Journey

As we move forward, it is essential to embrace the cultural and social journey that unites generations. By recognizing and valuing the unique contributions of each generation, we can create a synergistic relationship that enhances our collective well-being. This journey requires openness, empathy, and a commitment to building bridges rather than walls.

Cultural and social synergy is not just an ideal but a practical pathway to a more inclusive and prosperous future. By fostering intergenerational understanding and collaboration, we can harness the full potential of our diverse cultural heritage and create a society where every generation has the opportunity to contribute, learn, and thrive. Let us celebrate our differences and come together to build a better world for all.

Exercise: Bridging Generational Gaps

Objective:

To enhance understanding and implementation of cultural and social synergy concepts by engaging in practical activities that foster intergenerational dialogue and collaboration.

Instructions:

1. Intergenerational Dialogue Session:

Activity:

- Organize a meeting with individuals from at least three different generations (e.g., Baby Boomers, Generation X, Millennials, Generation Z).
- Each participant should share a personal story or experience that highlights their cultural background and generational perspective.

Discussion Points:

- Identify common themes and unique differences in the shared stories.
- Discuss how these differences can be leveraged to create a richer, more inclusive environment.

Outcome:

- Write a brief summary of the session, highlighting key insights and any potential ideas for fostering generational synergy in your community or workplace.

2. Collaborative Project:

Activity:

Form a cross-generational team to work on a small project that requires collaboration. This could be a community service project, a workplace task, or a creative endeavor like a group art piece.
Assign roles based on each member's strengths and experiences.

Reflection:

- After completing the project, hold a debriefing session to discuss the collaboration process. What worked well? What challenges did you face?

Outcome:

- Document the project's progress and results. Reflect on how the diverse perspectives and skills of the team members contributed to the project's success.

3. Technology Sharing Workshop:

Activity:

- Host a workshop where younger generations teach older generations about a specific technology or digital tool, such as social media platforms, collaboration software, or smartphone apps.
- Conversely, have older generations share a traditional skill or cultural practice with younger participants.

Engagement:

- Ensure hands-on participation where both groups actively engage with the new skills being taught.

Outcome:

- Create a guide or tutorial based on what was taught during the workshop. Participants should also write a short reflection on what they learned and how it could be applied in their daily lives.

4. Cultural Inclusivity Audit:

Activity:

- Conduct an audit of your workplace, community center, or any organization you are part of to assess how culturally inclusive it is.

- Use a checklist to evaluate elements like representation of different generations, availability of intergenerational programs, and inclusivity in communication methods.

Action Plan:
- Based on the audit results, develop an action plan to improve cultural and social inclusivity. This could include implementing new programs, revising existing policies, or creating more inclusive communication strategies.

Outcome:
- Present the action plan to your organization's leadership or relevant stakeholders. Follow up to track the implementation and impact of your proposed changes.

5. Storytelling and Knowledge Sharing Circle:

Activity:
- Arrange a storytelling circle where participants from different generations share personal stories related to their professional or life experiences.
- Encourage each participant to highlight a lesson or piece of wisdom they gained from their story.

Documentation:
- Record the stories (with participants' permission) or have a designated note-taker capture the key points.

Outcome:

- Compile the stories into a booklet or digital archive that can be shared within your community or organization. Reflect on the shared wisdom and how it can be applied to current challenges or opportunities.

Evaluation:

- After completing the exercises, reflect on the following questions:
- ✓ How did these activities change your understanding of cultural and social synergy?
- ✓ What new insights did you gain about different generations?
- ✓ How can you apply what you've learned to foster better intergenerational relationships in your own life?
- ✓ What tangible changes or improvements resulted from these activities?

Share your reflections and any action plans with a mentor, peer group, or within your organization to promote continuous learning and improvement in fostering cultural and social synergy.

Chapter 7: Economic Interdependence

Economic interdependence is the backbone of modern society, intertwining the fates of different generations in ways that foster mutual growth and prosperity. In a world where the economy is a complex web of relationships, understanding and leveraging these connections is essential for building a future that benefits everyone. This chapter explores how different generations can work together economically, the benefits of such collaboration, and practical steps to achieve it.

Understanding Economic Interdependence

Economic interdependence refers to the mutual reliance between different groups, regions, or countries for goods, services, resources, and knowledge. This concept extends to generational interdependence, where each generation relies on the other for economic stability and growth. For instance, older generations often provide experience, capital, and mentorship, while younger generations bring innovation, labor, and new perspectives[1].

The interwoven economic relationships between generations are vital for sustaining economic health and fostering innovation. For example, retirees depend on the working-age population to support social security systems, while the younger workforce benefits from the investments and infrastructure established by previous generations[2].

The Role of Generations in Economic Interdependence

Each generation plays a unique role in the economic ecosystem. Baby Boomers, having accumulated wealth and experience, often serve as investors, mentors, and consumers[3]. Generation X, in their prime working years, drive productivity and innovation in the workforce[4]. Millennials, known for their technological prowess, contribute fresh ideas and entrepreneurial spirit[5]. Generation Z, just entering the workforce, brings digital native skills and a keen sense of social responsibility[6].

Recognizing these roles helps in understanding how generations can complement each other economically. For instance, the entrepreneurial ventures of Millennials and Gen Z can benefit immensely from the funding and mentorship of Baby Boomers and Gen X. Similarly, younger generations can drive the adoption of new technologies in industries traditionally dominated by older generations[7].

Benefits of Generational Economic Collaboration

1. **Enhanced Innovation and Productivity:**

   - Collaboration between generations fosters a blend of experience and innovation. Older generations provide the wisdom and strategic oversight, while younger generations offer new technologies and innovative approaches[8].

2. **Economic Stability:**

- Intergenerational economic support, such as social security systems and retirement funds, ensures economic stability. Younger workers contribute to these systems, which support the older population, creating a sustainable economic cycle[9].

3. **Knowledge Transfer:**

- Economic interdependence facilitates the transfer of knowledge and skills. Mentorship programs allow seasoned professionals to pass on their expertise to younger colleagues, enhancing their career development[10].

4. **Investment in Future Generations:**

- Older generations investing in education, healthcare, and infrastructure benefits society as a whole, creating opportunities for the younger population and ensuring long-term economic growth[11].

Practical Steps to Foster Economic Interdependence

1. **Mentorship and Apprenticeship Programs:**

- Establish mentorship and apprenticeship programs within organizations to facilitate knowledge transfer and skill development. Encourage older employees to mentor younger ones, creating a culture of continuous learning[12].

2. **Intergenerational Business Ventures:**

- Promote the formation of business ventures that leverage the strengths of different generations. For example, a tech startup founded by Millennials could benefit from the strategic oversight and funding from Baby Boomers or Gen X investors[13].

3. **Inclusive Financial Policies:**

- Advocate for financial policies that support all generations, such as affordable education loans, retirement savings plans, and healthcare benefits. These policies should ensure that each generation can contribute to and benefit from economic growth[14].

4. **Community-Based Economic Initiatives:**

- Develop community-based economic initiatives that involve multiple generations. Examples include local businesses, cooperatives, and community investment projects. These initiatives can create jobs, stimulate local economies, and foster a sense of community[15].

5. **Technology Integration:**

- Encourage older generations to embrace new technologies through training and support. This integration can enhance productivity and open up new economic opportunities. Similarly, younger generations should respect and learn from traditional business practices and ethics[16].

6. **Lifelong Learning:**

- Promote a culture of lifelong learning where individuals continually update their skills and knowledge. This can be achieved through professional development programs, online courses, and workshops tailored to different age groups[17].

Case Studies of Economic Interdependence

Case Study 1: Intergenerational Startups A tech startup, founded by a group of Millennials, partners with Baby Boomers for investment and strategic guidance. The Baby Boomers, with their extensive business experience, help the startup navigate the complexities of the market, while the Millennials drive innovation and technological development. This collaboration results in a successful business that benefits both generations[18].

Case Study 2: Community Investment Projects In a small town, a group of retirees invests in a community center that offers after-school programs for children and job training for young adults. The community center becomes a hub for economic activity, creating jobs and providing valuable services. The retirees see a return on their investment through the revitalization of their community and the economic opportunities created for younger generations[19].

The Path Forward

Embracing economic interdependence requires a shift in mindset. We must move away from viewing generations as isolated groups with conflicting interests and towards seeing them as interdependent partners in economic growth. This shift involves fostering collaboration, creating inclusive policies, and investing in initiatives that benefit all generations[20].

By recognizing and leveraging the unique strengths of each generation, we can create a more dynamic and resilient economy. This approach not only enhances economic stability and growth but also builds a society where everyone, regardless of age, can thrive and contribute meaningfully[21].

In conclusion, economic interdependence is a powerful concept that can drive mutual growth, success, and prosperity. By fostering intergenerational collaboration, we can harness the full potential of our diverse economic ecosystem, ensuring a brighter future for all generations. Let us embrace this interdependence and work together to build a stronger, more inclusive economy[22].

Exercise: Building Economic Bridges Across Generations

Objective:

To enhance the reader's understanding and practical application of economic interdependence concepts by engaging in activities that foster intergenerational collaboration and economic growth.

Instructions:

1. Intergenerational Mentorship Match:

- **Activity:**
  - ✓ Identify a mentor from an older generation and a mentee from a younger generation within your organization or community.
  - ✓ Establish a mentorship relationship where both parties commit to regular meetings over a three-month period.

- **Discussion Points:**
  - ✓ Set clear goals for what both the mentor and mentee hope to achieve.
  - ✓ Encourage the mentor to share insights on strategic thinking and long-term planning.
  - ✓ Have the mentee introduce new technologies or innovative practices relevant to the mentor's interests.

- **Outcome:**

✓ At the end of the three months, both the mentor and mentee should write a reflection on what they have learned and how it has impacted their personal and professional growth.

2. **Cross-Generational Business Plan:**

- **Activity:**
  ✓ Form a team that includes members from at least three different generations.
  ✓ Collaboratively develop a business plan for a new venture that leverages the strengths and perspectives of each generation.
- **Tasks:**
✓ Conduct market research to identify a business opportunity that appeals to a broad audience.
✓ Develop a financial plan that includes funding strategies and potential revenue streams.
✓ Create a marketing strategy that incorporates both traditional and digital channels.

- **Outcome:**
✓ Present the business plan to a panel of advisors or potential investors, receiving feedback on its viability and potential for success.

3.   **Economic Policy Advocacy:**

- **Activity:**
  - ✓ Research current economic policies that affect different generations, such as retirement benefits, student loans, and healthcare.
  - ✓ Formulate a policy proposal that aims to enhance economic interdependence and support all generations.

- **Steps:**
  - ✓ Identify key stakeholders who can influence policy changes.
  - ✓ Develop a comprehensive proposal that includes background information, proposed changes, and expected outcomes.
  - ✓ Organize a campaign to advocate for the proposed policy, including writing letters to policymakers, engaging with the media, and organizing community events.

- **Outcome:**
  - ✓ Measure the impact of your advocacy efforts by tracking responses from policymakers and changes in public opinion.

4.   Community Investment Project:

✓ **Activity:**
✓ Identify a community project that can benefit from intergenerational collaboration, such as a local park renovation, a community garden, or a youth education program.
✓ Recruit volunteers from various generations to participate in the project.

• **Steps:**
✓ Plan the project, including the necessary resources, timeline, and roles for each volunteer.
✓ Execute the project, ensuring that each generation has the opportunity to contribute their skills and knowledge.

• **Outcome:**
✓ Document the project's progress and results through photos, videos, and written reports.
✓ Host a community event to celebrate the project's completion and acknowledge the contributions of all volunteers.

5. Technology Training Exchange:

- **Activity:**
  - ✓ Organize a series of workshops where younger generations teach older generations how to use new technologies (e.g., social media, smartphones, or software applications) and older generations share traditional skills (e.g., craftsmanship, cooking, or gardening).

- **Steps:**
  - ✓ Identify the skills and technologies to be exchanged.
  - ✓ Schedule workshops and ensure that they are accessible to participants from all generations.
  - ✓ Encourage interactive participation and hands-on learning.

- **Outcome:**
  - ✓ Create a guide or booklet based on the workshops, capturing the knowledge shared and the experiences of the participants.
  - ✓ Conduct follow-up sessions to see how participants have applied their new skills.

Evaluation:

- After completing the exercises, reflect on the following questions:

✓ How did these activities enhance your understanding of economic interdependence?

✓ What new insights did you gain about the economic contributions of different generations?

✓ How can you apply what you've learned to foster better economic collaboration in your own life?

✓ What tangible changes or improvements resulted from these activities?

Share your reflections and any action plans with a mentor, peer group, or within your organization to promote continuous learning and improvement in fostering economic interdependence.

Chapter 8: Emotional and Psychological Bonds

In the intricate tapestry of human relationships, emotional and psychological bonds form the threads that weave generations together. These bonds are the unseen yet profoundly felt connections that foster understanding, empathy, and unity across ages. This chapter delves into the significance of emotional and psychological bonds between generations, exploring how they contribute to mutual growth, success, and prosperity, and offering practical strategies to strengthen these vital connections.

The Essence of Emotional and Psychological Bonds

Emotional and psychological bonds are foundational to human interactions. They are built on trust, mutual respect, and shared experiences. These bonds transcend the barriers of age, allowing for meaningful relationships that enrich the lives of all involved. When generations connect on an emotional level, they can share wisdom, provide support, and cultivate a sense of belonging[1].

The interplay between different generations' emotional and psychological needs is crucial for fostering a cohesive society. Younger generations seek guidance and mentorship, while older generations find purpose and joy in passing on their knowledge. This reciprocal relationship enhances the well-being of both parties, creating a nurturing environment where everyone can thrive[2].

The Impact of Emotional Bonds on Generational Unity

Emotional bonds are the glue that holds families and communities together. They play a critical role in bridging generational gaps and fostering a sense of unity. For instance, the bond between grandparents and grandchildren is often characterized by unconditional love and support. This relationship can provide children with a strong sense of security and identity, while giving grandparents a renewed sense of purpose[3].

In a broader societal context, emotional bonds between generations can lead to greater social cohesion. When individuals of different ages engage in open and empathetic communication, they break down stereotypes and build mutual respect. This can lead to collaborative efforts that address community issues, create inclusive policies, and promote social harmony[4].

The Role of Psychological Bonds in Intergenerational Relationships

Psychological bonds complement emotional connections by fostering a deeper understanding of each generation's unique perspectives and experiences. These bonds are nurtured through shared values, common goals, and mutual respect. By acknowledging and appreciating the psychological dimensions of intergenerational relationships, we can create environments that support mental and emotional well-being[5].

For example, mentorship programs in workplaces and educational institutions can create psychological bonds between younger and older participants. These programs enable the transfer of knowledge and skills, while also promoting a culture of continuous learning and growth. Mentors and mentees can develop strong psychological connections that enhance their professional and personal development[6].

Strengthening Emotional and Psychological Bonds

1. **Storytelling and Shared Experiences:**

   - Storytelling is a powerful tool for building emotional and psychological bonds. Encourage older generations to share their life stories, experiences, and lessons learned with younger family members or colleagues. These narratives can provide valuable insights and foster a deeper understanding of different life stages[7].
   - Practical Tip: Organize regular family gatherings or community events where storytelling is a central activity. Record these stories to preserve them for future generations.

2. **Intergenerational Activities:**

   - Engaging in activities that involve multiple generations can strengthen emotional bonds. Activities such as gardening, cooking, or volunteering together provide opportunities for meaningful interactions and shared experiences[8].

- Practical Tip: Create intergenerational programs in schools, community centers, or workplaces that encourage collaborative projects and activities.

3. **Open Communication:**

- Foster an environment where open communication is encouraged and valued. Ensure that individuals feel safe to express their thoughts, feelings, and concerns without fear of judgment[9].
- Practical Tip: Implement regular family meetings or team check-ins where everyone has a chance to speak and be heard.

4. **Mutual Support and Mentorship:**

- Encourage mutual support and mentorship between generations. Older individuals can offer guidance and advice, while younger individuals can provide assistance with new technologies or contemporary challenges[10].
- Practical Tip: Establish formal mentorship programs in organizations, pairing younger employees with more experienced mentors.

5. **Emotional Intelligence Development:**

- Promote the development of emotional intelligence (EI) across all generations. EI involves the ability to recognize, understand, and manage one's own emotions, as well as the emotions of others[11].

- Practical Tip: Offer workshops or training sessions on emotional intelligence in schools, workplaces, and community organizations.

Case Studies of Emotional and Psychological Bonding

Case Study 1: Family Storytelling Night A family initiated a weekly storytelling night where grandparents shared stories from their past with their grandchildren. This activity not only strengthened their emotional bonds but also provided the children with a sense of their family history and heritage. The grandparents felt valued and appreciated, while the children gained wisdom and understanding from their elders[12].

Case Study 2: Intergenerational Mentorship Program A corporation implemented an intergenerational mentorship program where younger employees were paired with older, more experienced mentors. The mentors provided guidance on career development and professional skills, while the younger employees introduced their mentors to new technologies and modern work practices. This program fostered mutual respect and created a supportive work environment[13].

The Path Forward

Strengthening emotional and psychological bonds between generations is essential for building a harmonious and prosperous society. By fostering these connections, we can create a supportive environment where individuals of all ages feel valued, understood, and empowered to contribute to the greater good[14].

As we move forward, it is crucial to prioritize activities and initiatives that promote intergenerational bonding. Whether through storytelling, shared activities, open communication, or mentorship, we must actively work to bridge the gaps between generations. This requires a commitment to empathy, respect, and continuous learning[15].

Emotional and psychological bonds are the foundation of generational unity. By nurturing these connections, we can create a society where all generations thrive together, drawing strength from their diversity and shared experiences. Let us embrace the power of emotional and psychological bonds to build a brighter, more connected future for all[16].

Exercise: Strengthening Emotional and Psychological Bonds

Objective:

To deepen the reader's understanding and practical implementation of emotional and psychological bonds between generations through activities that foster connection, empathy, and mutual growth.

Instructions:

1. **Family Storytelling Night:**

   - **Activity:**
   ✓ Organize a weekly storytelling night where family members of different generations share stories from their past.
   ✓ Ensure that each person gets an opportunity to share and listen.

   - **Tasks:**
   ✓ Prepare a list of themes or questions to guide the storytelling (e.g., "Describe a significant event in your life" or "What was your favorite childhood memory?").

   ✓ Record the stories (with permission) to create a family archive.

- **Outcome:**

   ✓ Strengthened emotional bonds through shared experiences and increased understanding of family history.

- **Evaluation:**

   ✓ Reflect on how the storytelling sessions have affected your relationships with family members. Write a brief summary of the most impactful stories and their lessons.

2. **Intergenerational Community Project:**

- **Activity:**

✓ Develop a community project that involves collaboration between different generations (e.g., a community garden, charity event, or local history project).

- **Steps:**

✓ Form a diverse team with members from various age groups.

✓ Plan the project, assigning roles and responsibilities that leverage the strengths of each generation.

✓ Execute the project and document its progress.

- **Outcome:**

✓ Enhanced community cohesion and mutual respect through collaborative efforts.

- **Evaluation:**

✓ After the project's completion, gather feedback from participants on their experiences. Reflect on how the project facilitated intergenerational connections and write a summary of its impact.

3. **Digital Literacy and Tech Mentorship:**

- **Activity:**

✓ Organize a series of workshops where younger individuals teach older adults how to use new technologies (e.g., smartphones, social media, video conferencing tools).

- **Steps:**

✓ Identify common technological needs and interests of older participants.

- ✓ Pair tech-savvy youth with older adults for personalized, hands-on learning sessions.

- ✓ Provide follow-up support and resources.

- **Outcome:**

- ✓ Increased digital literacy and confidence among older adults, fostering a sense of achievement and connection with younger generations.

- **Evaluation:**

- ✓ Measure the improvement in digital skills and gather feedback on the workshops' effectiveness. Write a report on the most significant benefits observed.

4. **Intergenerational Dialogue Circles:**

- **Activity:**

- ✓ Host regular dialogue circles where people from different generations discuss various topics, such as life experiences, societal changes, and future aspirations.

- **Steps:**

- ✓ Set up a comfortable, inclusive environment for open discussion.

- ✓ Choose discussion topics that resonate with all participants.

- ✓ Encourage respectful listening and sharing of perspectives.

- **Outcome:**

- ✓ Greater empathy and understanding between generations, breaking down stereotypes and building mutual respect.

- **Evaluation:**

- ✓ Reflect on the discussions and note any changes in attitudes or perceptions. Summarize key insights and how they have influenced your view of other generations.

5. **Emotional Intelligence Development Workshops:**

- **Activity:**

✓ Offer workshops on developing emotional intelligence (EI) across all generations.

- **Steps:**

✓ Design the workshops to include interactive activities, discussions, and practical exercises on recognizing and managing emotions.

✓ Include topics such as empathy, active listening, conflict resolution, and stress management.

- **Outcome:**

✓ Improved emotional intelligence, leading to better relationships and communication between generations.

- **Evaluation:**

✓ Assess participants' progress through pre- and post-workshop surveys. Write a reflection on the workshops' impact on your emotional intelligence and interpersonal relationships.

Evaluation:

- **Post-Exercise Reflection:**

✓ Reflect on how these activities have enhanced your understanding of emotional and psychological bonds.

✓ Consider what new insights you gained about the needs and contributions of different generations.

✓ Identify specific changes or improvements in your relationships and community dynamics as a result of these activities.

- **Sharing Insights:**

✓ Share your reflections and any action plans with a mentor, peer group, or within your organization to promote continuous learning and improvement in fostering intergenerational bonds.

By engaging in these exercises, readers can practically apply the concepts discussed in the chapter, leading to stronger, more empathetic, and collaborative intergenerational relationships.

NOTES:

Chapter 9: The Path Forward

As we stand on the brink of an era defined by unprecedented technological advancement, social evolution, and economic transformation, the importance of intergenerational unity has never been more critical. The path forward involves harnessing the collective wisdom, energy, and creativity of all generations to foster a society that thrives on mutual growth, success, and prosperity. This chapter outlines a comprehensive roadmap for achieving this vision, emphasizing actionable strategies that individuals, communities, and institutions can adopt to bridge generational divides and cultivate a harmonious, productive future.

Embracing Intergenerational Collaboration

The cornerstone of our path forward is the recognition and embrace of intergenerational collaboration. By leveraging the unique strengths and perspectives of each generation, we can create synergies that drive innovation and social cohesion. This requires a commitment to fostering environments where individuals of all ages feel valued and included.

1. **Create Inclusive Workplaces:**

- Organizations should strive to create workplaces that value diversity of age and experience. This includes implementing policies that encourage mentorship programs, reverse mentorship, and cross-functional teams that bring together employees from different generations[1].

- Practical Tip: Introduce intergenerational team projects and regular knowledge-sharing sessions to promote understanding and collaboration.

2. **Promote Lifelong Learning:**

   - Lifelong learning is essential for adapting to the rapid pace of change in today's world. Encouraging continuous education and skill development across all age groups ensures that everyone remains relevant and capable of contributing to their fullest potential[2].
   - Practical Tip: Offer accessible training programs and educational resources that cater to different learning preferences and technological proficiencies.

Building Stronger Community Ties

Communities are the fabric of our society, and strengthening intergenerational bonds within them is crucial for fostering social harmony and resilience. By creating opportunities for generations to interact and collaborate, we can build communities that are more inclusive and supportive.

1. **Develop Intergenerational Community Programs:**

   - Community centers, schools, and local organizations should develop programs that facilitate intergenerational engagement. This can include volunteer projects, cultural events, and recreational activities that bring together people of all ages[3].

- Practical Tip: Establish community gardens, art projects, or tech workshops that encourage collaboration between different generations.

2. **Foster Open Communication:**

- Open and honest communication is vital for understanding and appreciating the perspectives of different generations. Creating forums for dialogue and storytelling helps break down stereotypes and build mutual respect[4].

- Practical Tip: Organize regular intergenerational dialogue sessions or storytelling nights where community members can share their experiences and learn from each other.

Leveraging Technology for Connection

Technology can be a powerful tool for bridging generational gaps if used thoughtfully. By leveraging digital platforms to foster connection and collaboration, we can ensure that technological advancements benefit all generations.

1. **Encourage Digital Literacy:**

- Promoting digital literacy across all age groups is essential for ensuring that everyone can participate in the digital economy and stay connected. This includes providing training and resources to help older generations become more comfortable with technology[5].

- Practical Tip: Set up digital literacy workshops in community centers and libraries, pairing tech-savvy youth with older adults for hands-on learning.

2. **Utilize Social Media for Good:**

- Social media platforms can be used to promote positive intergenerational interactions and share valuable information. Encourage the use of these platforms to celebrate achievements, share knowledge, and build supportive online communities[6].
- Practical Tip: Create community social media groups that focus on sharing success stories, community events, and opportunities for intergenerational engagement.

Policy and Institutional Support

Achieving intergenerational unity requires support from policies and institutions that prioritize the well-being of all age groups. By advocating for and implementing policies that support intergenerational collaboration, we can create a more equitable and thriving society.

1. **Implement Inclusive Policies:**

- Governments and organizations should develop policies that support the needs of all generations. This includes fair employment practices, affordable education and healthcare, and social security systems that ensure financial stability for the elderly[7].

- Practical Tip: Advocate for policies that promote flexible work arrangements, caregiver support, and affordable lifelong education programs.

2. **Promote Intergenerational Housing:**

- Housing policies that encourage intergenerational living arrangements can foster closer family ties and mutual support. This includes designing communities that accommodate the needs of both young families and older adults[8].
- Practical Tip: Support initiatives that provide affordable housing options for multi-generational families and develop community spaces that encourage intergenerational interaction.

Cultivating a Culture of Empathy and Respect

At the heart of intergenerational unity is a culture of empathy and respect. By fostering these values, we can create a society where every individual feels valued and supported, regardless of their age.

1. **Encourage Empathy Through Education:**

- Educational institutions play a crucial role in teaching empathy and respect. By incorporating these values into the curriculum, we can nurture a generation of individuals who are compassionate and understanding[9].

- Practical Tip: Introduce programs in schools that focus on emotional intelligence, conflict resolution, and the importance of diversity and inclusion.

2. **Celebrate Generational Contributions:**

- Recognizing and celebrating the contributions of different generations helps build a culture of appreciation and respect. This includes honoring the achievements of older generations while also valuing the innovations brought by younger ones[10].
- Practical Tip: Organize community events that highlight the accomplishments of individuals from different generations, such as award ceremonies, exhibitions, and public acknowledgments.

Moving Forward Together

The path forward is one of shared effort and mutual benefit. By embracing intergenerational collaboration, building stronger community ties, leveraging technology, advocating for inclusive policies, and cultivating a culture of empathy and respect, we can create a society where every generation thrives. This journey requires dedication, openness, and a commitment to working together for the greater good.

As we move forward, let us remember that the strength of our society lies in its diversity. Each generation brings unique strengths, experiences, and perspectives that, when united, can drive profound growth and prosperity. Together, we can build a future that honors our past, embraces the present, and looks forward to a brighter, more connected tomorrow.

Let us embark on this path forward with hope, determination, and a shared vision of a united, thriving, and prosperous society for all generations[11].

Exercise: Implementing Intergenerational Collaboration

Objective:

To enhance the reader's understanding and practical application of intergenerational collaboration by engaging in activities that foster connection, empathy, and mutual growth across different generations.

Instructions:

1. **Intergenerational Mentorship Program:**

- **Activity:**

✓ Pair up with a mentor from a different generation within your organization or community.

✓ Establish a regular meeting schedule over three months, focusing on mutual learning and support.

- **Tasks:**

✓ The younger participant introduces the mentor to a new technology or digital tool.

✓ The older participant shares insights and experiences related to professional or personal development.

- **Outcome:**

- ✓ Write a reflection on what each party learned from the experience and how it impacted their personal and professional growth.

- **Evaluation:**

- ✓ Assess how the mentorship program has enhanced your skills, knowledge, and understanding of different generational perspectives.

2. **Community Project Collaboration:**

- **Activity:**

- ✓ Identify a community project that requires collaboration between different generations, such as a community garden, local charity event, or neighborhood improvement initiative.

- **Steps:**

- ✓ Form a diverse team with members from various age groups.

- ✓ Develop a project plan that outlines goals, tasks, and timelines.

- ✓ Work together to execute the project, ensuring active participation from all team members.

- **Outcome:**

- ✓ Document the project's progress with photos, videos, and written reports.

- ✓ Host a community event to showcase the project and celebrate the contributions of all generations involved.

- **Evaluation:**

- ✓ Reflect on the success of the project and how intergenerational collaboration contributed to achieving the goals. Gather feedback from participants on their experiences.

3. **Digital Literacy Workshop:**

- **Activity:**

  ✓ Organize a series of workshops where tech-savvy youth teach older adults how to use new technologies, such as smartphones, social media, or video conferencing tools.

- **Steps:**

  ✓ Plan the workshop content based on the interests and needs of the older participants.

  ✓ Conduct hands-on sessions that allow participants to practice using the technology.

  ✓ Provide follow-up support to ensure participants are comfortable and confident with their new skills.

- **Outcome:**

  ✓ Create a guide or tutorial based on the workshop content, which can be shared with the wider community.

  ✓ Encourage participants to form a support network where they can continue to learn and assist each other.

- **Evaluation:**

  ✓ Measure the increase in digital literacy and confidence among the older participants. Collect feedback on the effectiveness of the workshops.

4. **Intergenerational Storytelling Event:**

- **Activity:**

  ✓ Host an event where individuals from different generations share personal stories, experiences, and lessons learned.

- **Steps:**

  ✓ Invite community members of all ages to participate and share their stories.

✓ Create a comfortable and inclusive environment for storytelling.

✓ Record the stories (with permission) to preserve them for future generations.

- **Outcome:**

✓ Compile the stories into a booklet or digital archive that can be shared within the community.

✓ Use the event as an opportunity to promote understanding and empathy between generations.

- **Evaluation:**

✓ Reflect on the themes and lessons that emerged from the stories. Assess how the event has strengthened emotional and psychological bonds within the community.

5. **Policy Advocacy Campaign:**

- **Activity:**

✓ Develop a campaign to advocate for policies that support intergenerational collaboration and inclusivity.

- **Steps:**

✓ Research existing policies and identify areas that need improvement.

✓ Create a proposal that outlines specific policy changes and their benefits.

✓ Organize a series of events, such as town hall meetings or online forums, to gather support and raise awareness.

- **Outcome:**

✓ Present the proposal to local policymakers and stakeholders.

✓ Track the progress of the campaign and any changes that result from it.

- **Evaluation:**

✓ Evaluate the impact of the advocacy campaign on policy changes and community support. Gather feedback from participants on the campaign's effectiveness.

Exercise Evaluation:

- After completing the exercises, reflect on the following questions:

✓ How did these activities enhance your understanding of intergenerational collaboration?

✓ What new insights did you gain about the contributions and perspectives of different generations?

✓ How can you apply what you've learned to foster better intergenerational relationships in your personal and professional life?

✓ What tangible changes or improvements resulted from these activities?

Share your reflections and any action plans with a mentor, peer group, or within your organization to promote continuous learning and improvement in fostering intergenerational collaboration.

NOTES:

Conclusion: Embracing Our Shared Journey

As we conclude this journey through the interconnectedness of generations, it becomes evident that each chapter in this book has woven a rich tapestry of insights, stories, and practical strategies. These elements highlight the immense potential that lies in bridging generational gaps. Our collective efforts to understand, respect, and leverage the unique strengths of each generation are crucial for building a harmonious, prosperous, and resilient society.

The Power of the Past

Understanding the past is crucial for shaping our future. Chapter 1 explored how the experiences and lessons of older generations provide a foundation upon which younger generations can build. The wisdom gleaned from history allows us to avoid past mistakes, honor enduring values, and innovate with a sense of continuity. As we move forward, it is essential to keep the power of the past alive in our memories and actions, ensuring that we remain grounded in our collective heritage.

Bridging the Gap

In Chapter 2, we delved into the strategies for bridging generational gaps. Open communication, empathy, and mutual respect are the cornerstones of this effort. By actively listening to each other's perspectives and valuing the contributions of all age groups, we can create a society where everyone feels included and empowered. Bridging the gap is not a one-time effort but an ongoing commitment to fostering understanding and collaboration across generations.

The Digital Natives

Chapter 3 highlighted the transformative influence of digital natives. The younger generation, adept at navigating the digital landscape, brings innovative solutions and fresh perspectives to the table. Their familiarity with technology can drive progress in various sectors, from business to education to healthcare. However, it is crucial for digital natives to remain open to learning from the experiences and insights of older generations, ensuring that technological advancements are grounded in wisdom and ethical considerations.

Collaborative Success

In Chapter 4, we explored the dynamics of collaborative success. By fostering intergenerational teams and encouraging cross-functional collaboration, we can harness diverse skills and perspectives. This synergy not only enhances productivity but also drives innovation. Collaborative success is achieved when individuals of different ages work together towards common goals, leveraging their unique strengths to overcome challenges and seize opportunities.

Wisdom Meets Innovation

Chapter 5 emphasized the power of combining wisdom with innovation. The experience and knowledge of older generations provide a stable foundation for the creative and often disruptive ideas of younger generations. This combination can lead to groundbreaking advancements and sustainable growth. It is through this fusion of old and new, traditional and modern, that we can navigate the complexities of the contemporary world and build a future that honors our past while embracing change.

Cultural and Social Synergy

In Chapter 6, we examined the importance of cultural and social synergy. Diversity is our strength, and by fostering environments where different cultural backgrounds and perspectives are valued, we can create richer, more inclusive communities. This cultural and social synergy enhances our collective well-being, promotes mutual respect, and drives social progress. By celebrating our differences and finding common ground, we build a more cohesive and vibrant society.

Economic Interdependence

Chapter 7 explored the concept of economic interdependence. Generational collaboration in economic activities ensures stability and growth. Older generations often provide capital, experience, and mentorship, while younger generations bring innovation, labor, and new market perspectives. This interdependence fosters a balanced and resilient economy where all generations contribute to and benefit from collective prosperity.

Emotional and Psychological Bonds

In Chapter 8, we delved into the significance of emotional and psychological bonds. These bonds, built on trust, respect, and shared experiences, are the glue that holds families and communities together. By nurturing these connections, we create supportive environments where individuals of all ages feel valued and understood. Emotional and psychological bonds are essential for fostering empathy, reducing loneliness, and enhancing overall well-being.

The Path Forward

Finally, Chapter 9 provided a roadmap for the future. Embracing intergenerational collaboration, building stronger community ties, leveraging technology, advocating for inclusive policies, and cultivating a culture of empathy and respect are the key steps on this path forward. This journey requires a collective commitment to continuous learning, open communication, and mutual support.

Embracing Our Shared Journey

As we reflect on the themes and insights of this book, it is clear that the journey towards generational unity is both challenging and rewarding. It requires us to step out of our comfort zones, challenge our assumptions, and actively engage with those who are different from us. By doing so, we unlock the potential for mutual growth, success, and prosperity.

The future is bright when we walk this path together, hand in hand, across generations. Let us embrace our shared journey with hope, determination, and a commitment to building a world where every generation thrives. In this interconnected world, our strength lies in our unity, and our success is built on the foundation of mutual respect, understanding, and collaboration.

As we move forward, let us remember that each generation has something valuable to offer. By embracing the power of our collective wisdom and energy, we can create a future that honors our past, enriches our present, and illuminates our path forward. Together, we can build a brighter, more connected, and more prosperous world for all.

NOTES:

Footnotes

Chapter 1: The Power of the Past

[1] Strauss, W., & Howe, N. (1991). Generations: The History of America's Future, 1584 to 2069. William Morrow & Company.

[2] Taylor, P., & Gao, G. (2014). The Next America: Boomers, Millennials, and the Looming Generational Showdown. PublicAffairs.

[3] Coupland, D. (1991). Generation X: Tales for an Accelerated Culture. St. Martin's Press.

[4] Tapscott, D. (2009). Grown Up Digital: How the Net Generation is Changing Your World. McGraw-Hill.

[5] Pew Research Center. (2010). Millennials: A Portrait of Generation Next. Retrieved from Pew Research.

[6] Winograd, M., & Hais, M. (2011). Millennial Momentum: How a New Generation Is Remaking America. Rutgers University Press.

[7] Twenge, J. M. (2017). iGen: Why Today's Super-Connected Kids Are Growing Up Less Rebellious, More Tolerant, Less Happy – and Completely Unprepared for Adulthood. Atria Books.

[8] Seemiller, C., & Grace, M. (2016). Generation Z Goes to College. Jossey-Bass.

[9] Brokaw, T. (1998). The Greatest Generation. Random House.

[10] Isserman, M., & Kazin, M. (2000). America Divided: The Civil War of the 1960s. Oxford University Press.

[11] Gladwell, M. (2000). The Tipping Point: How Little Things Can Make a Big Difference. Little, Brown and Company.

[12] McAdams, D. P. (1993). The Stories We Live By: Personal Myths and the Making of the Self. The Guilford Press.

[13] Kram, K. E. (1985). Mentoring at Work: Developmental Relationships in Organizational Life. University Press of America.

Chapter 2: Bridging the Gap

[1] Brokaw, T. (1998). The Greatest Generation. Random House.

[2] Taylor, P., & Gao, G. (2014). The Next America: Boomers, Millennials, and the Looming Generational Showdown. PublicAffairs.

[3] Coupland, D. (1991). Generation X: Tales for an Accelerated Culture. St. Martin's Press.

[4] Pew Research Center. (2010). Millennials: A Portrait of Generation Next. Retrieved from Pew Research.

[5] Twenge, J. M. (2017). iGen: Why Today's Super-Connected Kids Are Growing Up Less Rebellious, More Tolerant, Less Happy – and Completely Unprepared for Adulthood. Atria Books.

[6] Carnegie, D. (1990). How to Win Friends and Influence People. Pocket Books.

[7] Putnam, R. D. (2000). Bowling Alone: The Collapse and Revival of American Community. Simon & Schuster.

[8] Kram, K. E. (1985). Mentoring at Work: Developmental Relationships in Organizational Life. University Press of America.

[9] Senge, P. M. (1990). The Fifth Discipline: The Art and Practice of the Learning Organization. Doubleday.

[10] Hofstede, G. (2001). Culture's Consequences: Comparing Values, Behaviors, Institutions and Organizations Across Nations. Sage Publications.

[11] Goleman, D. (1995). Emotional Intelligence: Why It Can Matter More Than IQ. Bantam Books.

[12] Rogers, E. M. (2003). Diffusion of Innovations. Free Press.

[13] Kouzes, J. M., & Posner, B. Z. (2017). The Leadership Challenge: How to Make Extraordinary Things Happen in Organizations. Jossey-Bass.

[14] Clutterbuck, D. (2004). Everyone Needs a Mentor: Fostering Talent in Your Organization. Chartered Institute of Personnel and Development.

[15] Johnson, R. (2011). A History of the American People. Harper Perennial.

Chapter 3: The Digital Natives

[1] Prensky, M. (2001). Digital Natives, Digital Immigrants. On the Horizon, 9(5), 1-6.

[2] Tapscott, D. (2009). Grown Up Digital: How the Net Generation is Changing Your World. McGraw-Hill.

[3] Twenge, J. M. (2017). iGen: Why Today's Super-Connected Kids Are Growing Up Less Rebellious, More Tolerant, Less Happy – and Completely Unprepared for Adulthood. Atria Books.

[4] Seemiller, C., & Grace, M. (2016). Generation Z Goes to College. Jossey-Bass.

[5] Anderson, M., & Jiang, J. (2018). Teens, Social Media & Technology 2018. Pew Research Center.

[6] Deloitte. (2019). Global Millennial Survey 2019. Deloitte Insights.

[7] Barnes, K., Marateo, R. C., & Ferris, S. P. (2007). Teaching and Learning with the Net Generation. Innovate: Journal of Online Education, 3(4).

[8] Meister, J. C., & Willyerd, K. (2010). The 2020 Workplace: How Innovative Companies Attract, Develop, and Keep Tomorrow's Employees Today. HarperBusiness.

[9] Seemiller, C., & Grace, M. (2019). Generation Z: A Century in the Making. Routledge.

[10] Bennett, S., Maton, K., & Kervin, L. (2008). The 'Digital Natives' Debate: A Critical Review of the Evidence. British Journal of Educational Technology, 39(5), 775-786.

[11] Goleman, D. (1995). Emotional Intelligence: Why It Can Matter More Than IQ. Bantam Books.

[12] Cain, S. (2012). Quiet: The Power of Introverts in a World That Can't Stop Talking. Crown Publishing Group.

[13] Winograd, M., & Hais, M. D. (2011). Millennial Momentum: How a New Generation is Remaking America. Rutgers University Press.

[14] Shirky, C. (2008). Here Comes Everybody: The Power of Organizing Without Organizations. Penguin Press.

Chapter 4: Collaborative Success

[1] Sawyer, R. K. (2007). Group Genius: The Creative Power of Collaboration. Basic Books.

[2] Johnson, W. B., & Ridley, C. R. (2008). The Elements of Mentoring. Palgrave Macmillan.

[3] Page, S. E. (2007). The Difference: How the Power of Diversity Creates Better Groups, Firms, Schools, and Societies. Princeton University Press.

[4] Edmondson, A. C. (2012). Teamwork on the Fly. Harvard Business Review.

[5] Duhigg, C. (2016). Smarter Faster Better: The Secrets of Being Productive in Life and Business. Random House.

[6] Lencioni, P. (2002). The Five Dysfunctions of a Team: A Leadership Fable. Jossey-Bass.

[7] Tjosvold, D. (2008). The Conflict-Positive Organization: It Depends on Us. Journal of Organizational Behavior.

[8] Goleman, D. (1995). Emotional Intelligence: Why It Can Matter More Than IQ. Bantam Books.

[9] Tapscott, D. (2009). Grown Up Digital: How the Net Generation is Changing Your World. McGraw-Hill.

[10] Hofstede, G. (2001). Culture's Consequences: Comparing Values, Behaviors, Institutions and Organizations Across Nations. Sage Publications.

[11] Covey, S. R. (1989). The 7 Habits of Highly Effective People: Powerful Lessons in Personal Change. Free Press.

[12] Brown, B. (2018). Dare to Lead: Brave Work. Tough Conversations. Whole Hearts. Random House.

[13] Isaacs, W. (1999). Dialogue and the Art of Thinking Together: A Pioneering Approach to Communicating in Business and in Life. Currency.

[14] Buckingham, M., & Goodall, A. (2019). Nine Lies About Work: A Freethinking Leader's Guide to the Real World. Harvard Business Review Press.

[15] Christensen, C. M., Grossman, J. H., & Hwang, J. (2009). The Innovator's Prescription: A Disruptive Solution for Health Care. McGraw-Hill.

[16] Putnam, R. D. (2000). Bowling Alone: The Collapse and Revival of American Community. Simon & Schuster.

[17] Steele, C. M. (2010). Whistling Vivaldi: How Stereotypes Affect Us and What We Can Do. W. W. Norton & Company.

[18] McKee, A. (2015). Management: A Focus on Leaders. Pearson.

[19] Rogers, E. M. (2003). *Diffusion

Chapter 5: Wisdom Meets Innovation

[1] Tjosvold, D. (2008). The Conflict-Positive Organization: It Depends on Us. Journal of Organizational Behavior.

[2] Goleman, D. (1995). Emotional Intelligence: Why It Can Matter More Than IQ. Bantam Books.

[3] Putnam, R. D. (2000). Bowling Alone: The Collapse and Revival of American Community. Simon & Schuster.

[4] Tapscott, D. (2009). Grown Up Digital: How the Net Generation is Changing Your World. McGraw-Hill.

[5] Page, S. E. (2007). The Difference: How the Power of Diversity Creates Better Groups, Firms, Schools, and Societies. Princeton University Press.

[6] Anderson, M., & Jiang, J. (2018). Teens, Social Media & Technology 2018. Pew Research Center.

[7] Isaacs, W. (1999). Dialogue and the Art of Thinking Together: A Pioneering Approach to Communicating in Business and in Life. Currency.

[8] Johnson, W. B., & Ridley, C. R. (2008). The Elements of Mentoring. Palgrave Macmillan.

[9] Buckingham, M., & Goodall, A. (2019). Nine Lies About Work: A Freethinking Leader's Guide to the Real World. Harvard Business Review Press.

[10] Brown, B. (2018). Dare to Lead: Brave Work. Tough Conversations. Whole Hearts. Random House.

[11] Meister, J. C., & Willyerd, K. (2010). The 2020 Workplace: How Innovative Companies Attract, Develop, and Keep Tomorrow's Employees Today. HarperBusiness.

[12] Christensen, C. M., Grossman, J. H., & Hwang, J. (2009). The Innovator's Prescription: A Disruptive Solution for Health Care. McGraw-Hill.

[13] Steele, C. M. (2010). Whistling Vivaldi: How Stereotypes Affect Us and What We Can Do. W. W. Norton & Company.

[14] McKee, A. (2015). Management: A Focus on Leaders. Pearson.

[15] Rogers, E. M. (2003). Diffusion of Innovations. Free Press.

Chapter 6: Cultural and Social Synergy

[1] Howe, N., & Strauss, W. (2000). Millennials Rising: The Next Great Generation. Vintage Books.

[2] Pew Research Center. (2014). Millennials in Adulthood: Detached from Institutions, Networked with Friends.

[3] Williams, A., & Page, R. (2011). Marketing to the Generations. Journal of Behavioral Studies in Business, 3(1), 1-17.

[4] Anderson, M., & Jiang, J. (2018). Teens, Social Media & Technology 2018. Pew Research Center.

[5] British Library. (n.d.). Digital Preservation. Retrieved from British Library Digital Preservation

[6] Vanderbeck, R. M. (2007). Intergenerational Geographies: Age Relations, Segregation and Re-engagements. Geography Compass, 1(2), 200-221.

[7] Fivush, R. (2008). Remembering and Reminiscing: How Individual Lives are Constructed in Family Narratives. Memory Studies, 1(1), 49-58.

[8] Madden, M. (2010). Older Adults and Social Media. Pew Research Center.

[9] Harvard Business Review. (2014). Mentoring Millennials.

[10] Granville, G. (2002). A Review of Intergenerational Practice in the UK. Stoke-on-Trent: Beth Johnson Foundation.

[11] Banks, J. A. (2008). Diversity, Group Identity, and Citizenship Education in a Global Age. Educational Researcher, 37(3), 129-139.

[12] Kaplan, M. S., & Sanchez, M. (2014). Intergenerational Programs: Support for Children, Youth, and Elders in Japan. Springer Publishing Company.

[13] AARP. (2018). The Longevity Economy: How People Over 50 Are Driving Economic and Social Value in the US.

[14] Hewlett, S. A., Sherbin, L., & Sumberg, K. (2009). How Gen Y & Boomers Will Reshape Your Agenda. Harvard Business Review.

[15] United Nations. (2017). World Population Ageing 2017 Highlights.

Chapter 7: Economic Interdependence

[1] Samuelson, P. A., & Nordhaus, W. D. (2010). Economics. McGraw-Hill Education.

[2] Diamond, P. A., & Orszag, P. R. (2005). Saving Social Security: A Balanced Approach. Brookings Institution Press.

[3] Pew Research Center. (2015). The American Middle Class Is Losing Ground.

[4] U.S. Bureau of Labor Statistics. (2021). Employment Projections.

[5] Tapscott, D. (2009). Grown Up Digital: How the Net Generation is Changing Your World. McGraw-Hill.

[6] Twenge, J. M. (2017). iGen: Why Today's Super-Connected Kids Are Growing Up Less Rebellious, More Tolerant, Less Happy—and Completely Unprepared for Adulthood. Atria Books.

[7] Deloitte. (2020). Millennials and Gen Z: Deloitte Global Millennial Survey 2020.

[8] Harvard Business Review. (2014). The Collaborative Organization: How to Make Employee Networks Really Work.

[9] Social Security Administration. (2020). Annual Report of the Board of Trustees of the Federal Old-Age and Survivors Insurance and Federal Disability Insurance Trust Funds.

[10] Clutterbuck, D. (2004). Everyone Needs a Mentor: Fostering Talent in Your Organization. Chartered Institute of Personnel and Development.

[11] World Bank. (2019). World Development Report 2019: The Changing Nature of Work.

[12] Kram, K. E. (1985). Mentoring at Work: Developmental Relationships in Organizational Life. University Press of America.

[13] PwC. (2016). The Sharing Economy: Consumer Intelligence Series.

[14] OECD. (2017). Pensions at a Glance 2017: OECD and G20 Indicators.

[15] Putnam, R. D. (2000). Bowling Alone: The Collapse and Revival of American Community. Simon & Schuster.

[16] McKinsey & Company. (2020). The Next Normal: The Future of Work after COVID-19.

[17] Knowles, M. S. (1975). Self-Directed Learning: A Guide for Learners and Teachers. Association Press.

[18] Startup Genome. (2020). The Global Startup Ecosystem Report 2020.

[19] Rockefeller Foundation. (2015). The Value of Community Investment: A Framework for Measurement.

[20] UN Department of Economic and Social Affairs. (2020). World Social Report 2020: Inequality in a Rapidly Changing World.

[21] Schwab, K. (2016). The Fourth Industrial Revolution. Crown Business.

[22] IMF. (2019). World Economic Outlook: Global Manufacturing Downturn, Rising Trade Barriers.

Chapter 8: Emotional and Psychological Bonds

[1] Bowlby, J. (1988). A Secure Base: Parent-Child Attachment and Healthy Human Development. Basic Books.

[2] Erikson, E. H. (1963). Childhood and Society. Norton.

[3] Bengtson, V. L. (2001). Beyond the Nuclear Family: The Increasing Importance of Multigenerational Bonds. Journal of Marriage and Family, 63(1), 1-16.

[4] Putnam, R. D. (2000). Bowling Alone: The Collapse and Revival of American Community. Simon & Schuster.

[5] Ryff, C. D., & Singer, B. (2008). Know Thyself and Become What You Are: A Eudaimonic Approach to Psychological Well-Being. Journal of Happiness Studies, 9(1), 13-39.

[6] Kram, K. E. (1985). Mentoring at Work: Developmental Relationships in Organizational Life. University Press of America.

[7] McAdams, D. P. (1993). The Stories We Live By: Personal Myths and the Making of the Self. William Morrow.

[8] Kaplan, M. S., & Sanchez, M. (2014). Intergenerational Programs: Support for Children, Youth, and Elders in Japan. Springer Publishing Company.

[9] Rogers, C. R. (1961). On Becoming a Person: A Therapist's View of Psychotherapy. Houghton Mifflin.

[10] Clutterbuck, D. (2004). Everyone Needs a Mentor: Fostering Talent in Your Organization. Chartered Institute of Personnel and Development.

[11] Goleman, D. (1995). Emotional Intelligence: Why It Can Matter More Than IQ. Bantam Books.

[12] Fivush, R. (2008). Remembering and Reminiscing: How Individual Lives are Constructed in Family Narratives. Memory Studies, 1(1), 49-58.

[13] Harvard Business Review. (2014). The Best Mentoring Programs Know That It's a Two-Way Street. Harvard Business Review.

[14] Larkin, E., & Newman, S. (1997). Intergenerational Programs: Imperatives, Strategies, Impacts, Trends. Haworth Press.

[15] Schachter, S., & Singer, J. (1962). Cognitive, Social, and Physiological Determinants of Emotional State. Psychological Review, 69(5), 379-399.

[16] Berkman, L. F., & Glass, T. (2000). Social Integration, Social Networks, Social Support, and Health. In L. F. Berkman & I. Kawachi (Eds.), Social Epidemiology. Oxford University Press.

Chapter 9: The Path Forward

[1] Kram, K. E. (1985). Mentoring at Work: Developmental Relationships in Organizational Life. University Press of America.

[2] Knowles, M. S. (1975). Self-Directed Learning: A Guide for Learners and Teachers. Association Press.

[3] Putnam, R. D. (2000). Bowling Alone: The Collapse and Revival of American Community. Simon & Schuster.

[4] Rogers, C. R. (1961). On Becoming a Person: A Therapist's View of Psychotherapy. Houghton Mifflin.

[5] Tapscott, D. (2009). Grown Up Digital: How the Net Generation is Changing Your World. McGraw-Hill.

[6] Harvard Business Review. (2014). The Best Mentoring Programs Know That It's a Two-Way Street. Harvard Business Review.

[7] Diamond, P. A., & Orszag, P. R. (2005). Saving Social Security: A Balanced Approach. Brookings Institution Press.

[8] United Nations. (2020). World Social Report 2020: Inequality in a Rapidly Changing World. United Nations Department of Economic and Social Affairs.

[9] Goleman, D. (1995). Emotional Intelligence: Why It Can Matter More Than IQ. Bantam Books.

[10] Erikson, E. H. (1963). Childhood and Society. Norton.

[11] Schwab, K. (2016). The Fourth Industrial Revolution. Crown Business.

Bibliography

Chapter 1: The Power of the Past

1. Brokaw, T. (1998). The Greatest Generation. Random House.

2. Coupland, D. (1991). Generation X: Tales for an Accelerated Culture. St. Martin's Press.

3. Gladwell, M. (2000). The Tipping Point: How Little Things Can Make a Big Difference. Little, Brown and Company.

4. Isserman, M., & Kazin, M. (2000). America Divided: The Civil War of the 1960s. Oxford University Press.

5. Kram, K. E. (1985). Mentoring at Work: Developmental Relationships in Organizational Life. University Press of America.

6. McAdams, D. P. (1993). The Stories We Live By: Personal Myths and the Making of the Self. The Guilford Press.

7. Pew Research Center. (2010). Millennials: A Portrait of Generation Next. Retrieved from Pew Research.

8. Seemiller, C., & Grace, M. (2016). Generation Z Goes to College. Jossey-Bass.

9. Strauss, W., & Howe, N. (1991). Generations: The History of America's Future, 1584 to 2069. William Morrow & Company.

10. Tapscott, D. (2009). Grown Up Digital: How the Net Generation is Changing Your World. McGraw-Hill.

11. Taylor, P., & Gao, G. (2014). The Next America: Boomers, Millennials, and the Looming Generational Showdown. PublicAffairs.

12. Twenge, J. M. (2017). iGen: Why Today's Super-Connected Kids Are Growing Up Less Rebellious, More Tolerant, Less Happy – and Completely Unprepared for Adulthood. Atria Books.

13. Winograd, M., & Hais, M. (2011). Millennial Momentum: How a New Generation Is Remaking America. Rutgers University Press.

Chapter 2: Bridging the Gap

1. Brokaw, T. (1998). The Greatest Generation. Random House.

2. Carnegie, D. (1990). How to Win Friends and Influence People. Pocket Books.

3. Clutterbuck, D. (2004). Everyone Needs a Mentor: Fostering Talent in Your Organization. Chartered Institute of Personnel and Development.

4. Coupland, D. (1991). Generation X: Tales for an Accelerated Culture. St. Martin's Press.

5. Goleman, D. (1995). Emotional Intelligence: Why It Can Matter More Than IQ. Bantam Books.

6. Hofstede, G. (2001). Culture's Consequences: Comparing Values, Behaviors, Institutions and Organizations Across Nations. Sage Publications.

7. Johnson, R. (2011). A History of the American People. Harper Perennial.

8. Kram, K. E. (1985). Mentoring at Work: Developmental Relationships in Organizational Life. University Press of America.

9. Kouzes, J. M., & Posner, B. Z. (2017). The Leadership Challenge: How to Make Extraordinary Things Happen in Organizations. Jossey-Bass.

10. Pew Research Center. (2010). Millennials: A Portrait of Generation Next. Retrieved from Pew Research.

11. Putnam, R. D. (2000). Bowling Alone: The Collapse and Revival of American Community. Simon & Schuster.

12. Rogers, E. M. (2003). Diffusion of Innovations. Free Press.

13. Senge, P. M. (1990). The Fifth Discipline: The Art and Practice of the Learning Organization. Doubleday.

14. Taylor, P., & Gao, G. (2014). The Next America: Boomers, Millennials, and the Looming Generational Showdown. PublicAffairs.

15. Twenge, J. M. (2017). iGen: Why Today's Super-Connected Kids Are Growing Up Less Rebellious, More Tolerant, Less Happy – and Completely Unprepared for Adulthood. Atria Books.

Chapter 3: The Digital Natives

1. Anderson, M., & Jiang, J. (2018). Teens, Social Media & Technology 2018. Pew Research Center.

2. Barnes, K., Marateo, R. C., & Ferris, S. P. (2007). Teaching and Learning with the Net Generation. Innovate: Journal of Online Education, 3(4).

3. Bennett, S., Maton, K., & Kervin, L. (2008). The 'Digital Natives' Debate: A Critical Review of the Evidence. British Journal of Educational Technology, 39(5), 775-786.

4. Cain, S. (2012). Quiet: The Power of Introverts in a World That Can't Stop Talking. Crown Publishing Group.

5. Deloitte. (2019). Global Millennial Survey 2019. Deloitte Insights.

6. Goleman, D. (1995). Emotional Intelligence: Why It Can Matter More Than IQ. Bantam Books.

7. Meister, J. C., & Willyerd, K. (2010). The 2020 Workplace: How Innovative Companies Attract, Develop, and Keep Tomorrow's Employees Today. HarperBusiness.

8. Prensky, M. (2001). Digital Natives, Digital Immigrants. On the Horizon, 9(5), 1-6.

9. Seemiller, C., & Grace, M. (2016). Generation Z Goes to College. Jossey-Bass.

10. Seemiller, C., & Grace, M. (2019). Generation Z: A Century in the Making. Routledge.

11. Shirky, C. (2008). Here Comes Everybody: The Power of Organizing Without Organizations. Penguin Press.

12. Tapscott, D. (2009). Grown Up Digital: How the Net Generation is Changing Your World. McGraw-Hill.

13. Twenge, J. M. (2017). iGen: Why Today's Super-Connected Kids Are Growing Up Less Rebellious, More Tolerant, Less Happy – and Completely Unprepared for Adulthood. Atria Books.

14. Winograd, M., & Hais, M. D. (2011). Millennial Momentum: How a New Generation is Remaking America. Rutgers University Press.

Chapter 4: Collaborative Success

1. Brown, B. (2018). Dare to Lead: Brave Work. Tough Conversations. Whole Hearts. Random House.

2. Buckingham, M., & Goodall, A. (2019). Nine Lies About Work: A Freethinking Leader's Guide to the Real World. Harvard Business Review Press.

3. Christensen, C. M., Grossman, J. H., & Hwang, J. (2009). The Innovator's Prescription: A Disruptive Solution for Health Care. McGraw-Hill.

4. Covey, S. R. (1989). The 7 Habits of Highly Effective People: Powerful Lessons in Personal Change. Free Press.

5. Duhigg, C. (2016). Smarter Faster Better: The Secrets of Being Productive in Life and Business. Random House.

6. Edmondson, A. C. (2012). Teamwork on the Fly. Harvard Business Review.

7. Goleman, D. (1995). Emotional Intelligence: Why It Can Matter More Than IQ. Bantam Books.

8. Hofstede, G. (2001). Culture's Consequences: Comparing Values, Behaviors, Institutions and Organizations Across Nations. Sage Publications.

9. Isaacs, W. (1999). Dialogue and the Art of Thinking Together: A Pioneering Approach to Communicating in Business and in Life. Currency.

10. Johnson, W. B., & Ridley, C. R. (2008). The Elements of Mentoring. Palgrave Macmillan.

11. Lencioni, P. (2002). The Five Dysfunctions of a Team: A Leadership Fable. Jossey-Bass.

12. McKee, A. (2015). Management: A Focus on Leaders. Pearson.

13. Page, S. E. (2007). The Difference: How the Power of Diversity Creates Better Groups, Firms, Schools, and Societies. Princeton University Press.

14. Putnam, R. D. (2000). Bowling Alone: The Collapse and Revival of American Community. Simon & Schuster.

15. Rogers, E. M. (2003). Diffusion of Innovations. Free Press.

16. Sawyer, R. K. (2007). Group Genius: The Creative Power of Collaboration. Basic Books.

17. Steele, C. M. (2010). Whistling Vivaldi: How Stereotypes Affect Us and What We Can Do. W. W. Norton & Company.

18. Tapscott, D. (2009). Grown Up Digital: How the Net Generation is Changing Your World. McGraw-Hill.

19. Tjosvold, D. (2008). The Conflict-Positive Organization: It Depends on Us. Journal of Organization

Chapter 5: Wisdom Meets Innovation

1. Anderson, M., & Jiang, J. (2018). Teens, Social Media & Technology 2018. Pew Research Center.

2. Brown, B. (2018). Dare to Lead: Brave Work. Tough Conversations. Whole Hearts. Random House.

3. Buckingham, M., & Goodall, A. (2019). Nine Lies About Work: A Freethinking Leader's Guide to the Real World. Harvard Business Review Press.

4. Christensen, C. M., Grossman, J. H., & Hwang, J. (2009). The Innovator's Prescription: A Disruptive Solution for Health Care. McGraw-Hill.

5. Goleman, D. (1995). Emotional Intelligence: Why It Can Matter More Than IQ. Bantam Books.

6. Isaacs, W. (1999). Dialogue and the Art of Thinking Together: A Pioneering Approach to Communicating in Business and in Life. Currency.

7. Johnson, W. B., & Ridley, C. R. (2008). The Elements of Mentoring. Palgrave Macmillan.

8. McKee, A. (2015). Management: A Focus on Leaders. Pearson.

9. Meister, J. C., & Willyerd, K. (2010). The 2020 Workplace: How Innovative Companies Attract, Develop, and Keep Tomorrow's Employees Today. HarperBusiness.

10. Page, S. E. (2007). The Difference: How the Power of Diversity Creates Better Groups, Firms, Schools, and Societies. Princeton University Press.

11. Putnam, R. D. (2000). Bowling Alone: The Collapse and Revival of American Community. Simon & Schuster.

12. Rogers, E. M. (2003). Diffusion of Innovations. Free Press.

13. Steele, C. M. (2010). Whistling Vivaldi: How Stereotypes Affect Us and What We Can Do. W. W. Norton & Company.

14. Tapscott, D. (2009). Grown Up Digital: How the Net Generation is Changing Your World. McGraw-Hill.

15. Tjosvold, D. (2008). The Conflict-Positive Organization: It Depends on Us. Journal of Organizational Behavior.

Chapter 6: Cultural and Social Synergy

1. Howe, N., & Strauss, W. (2000). Millennials Rising: The Next Great Generation. Vintage Books.

2. Pew Research Center. (2014). Millennials in Adulthood: Detached from Institutions, Networked with Friends.

3. Williams, A., & Page, R. (2011). Marketing to the Generations. Journal of Behavioral Studies in Business, 3(1), 1-17.

4. Anderson, M., & Jiang, J. (2018). Teens, Social Media & Technology 2018. Pew Research Center.

5. British Library. (n.d.). Digital Preservation. Retrieved from https://www.bl.uk/digital-preservation...

6. Vanderbeck, R. M. (2007). Intergenerational Geographies: Age Relations, Segregation and Re-engagements. Geography Compass, 1(2), 200-221.

7. Fivush, R. (2008). Remembering and Reminiscing: How Individual Lives are Constructed in Family Narratives. Memory Studies, 1(1), 49-58.

8. Madden, M. (2010). Older Adults and Social Media. Pew Research Center.

9. Harvard Business Review. (2014). Mentoring Millennials.

10. Granville, G. (2002). A Review of Intergenerational Practice in the UK. Stoke-on-Trent: Beth Johnson Foundation.

11. Banks, J. A. (2008). Diversity, Group Identity, and Citizenship Education in a Global Age. Educational Researcher, 37(3), 129-139.

12. Kaplan, M. S., & Sanchez, M. (2014). Intergenerational Programs: Support for Children, Youth, and Elders in Japan. Springer Publishing Company.

13. AARP. (2018). The Longevity Economy: How People Over 50 Are Driving Economic and Social Value in the US.

14. Hewlett, S. A., Sherbin, L., & Sumberg, K. (2009). How Gen Y & Boomers Will Reshape Your Agenda. Harvard Business Review.

15. United Nations. (2017). World Population Ageing 2017 Highlights.

Chapter 7: Economic Interdependence

1. Samuelson, P. A., & Nordhaus, W. D. (2010). Economics. McGraw-Hill Education.

2. Diamond, P. A., & Orszag, P. R. (2005). Saving Social Security: A Balanced Approach. Brookings Institution Press.

3, Pew Research Center. (2015). The American Middle Class Is Losing Ground.

4. U.S. Bureau of Labor Statistics. (2021). Employment Projections.

5. Tapscott, D. (2009). Grown Up Digital: How the Net Generation is Changing Your World. McGraw-Hill.

6. Twenge, J. M. (2017). iGen: Why Today's Super-Connected Kids Are Growing Up Less Rebellious, More Tolerant, Less Happy–and Completely Unprepared for Adulthood. Atria Books.

7. Deloitte. (2020). Millennials and Gen Z: Deloitte Global Millennial Survey 2020.

8. Harvard Business Review. (2014). The Collaborative Organization: How to Make Employee Networks Really Work.

9. Social Security Administration. (2020). Annual Report of the Board of Trustees of the Federal Old-Age and Survivors Insurance and Federal Disability Insurance Trust Funds.

10. Clutterbuck, D. (2004). Everyone Needs a Mentor: Fostering Talent in Your Organization. Chartered Institute of Personnel and Development.

11. World Bank. (2019). World Development Report 2019: The Changing Nature of Work.

12. Kram, K. E. (1985). Mentoring at Work: Developmental Relationships in Organizational Life. University Press of America.

13. PwC. (2016). The Sharing Economy: Consumer Intelligence Series.

14. OECD. (2017). Pensions at a Glance 2017: OECD and G20 Indicators.

15. Putnam, R. D. (2000). Bowling Alone: The Collapse and Revival of American Community. Simon & Schuster.

16. McKinsey & Company. (2020). The Next Normal: The Future of Work after COVID-19.

17. Knowles, M. S. (1975). Self-Directed Learning: A Guide for Learners and Teachers. Association Press.

18. Startup Genome. (2020). The Global Startup Ecosystem Report 2020.

19. Rockefeller Foundation. (2015). The Value of Community Investment: A Framework for Measurement.

20. UN Department of Economic and Social Affairs. (2020). World Social Report 2020: Inequality in a Rapidly Changing World.

21. Schwab, K. (2016). The Fourth Industrial Revolution. Crown Business.

22. IMF. (2019). World Economic Outlook: Global Manufacturing Downturn, Rising Trade Barriers.

Chapter 8: Emotional and Psychological Bonds

1. Bowlby, J. (1988). A Secure Base: Parent-Child Attachment and Healthy Human Development. Basic Books.

2. Erikson, E. H. (1963). Childhood and Society. Norton.

3. Bengtson, V. L. (2001). Beyond the Nuclear Family: The Increasing Importance of Multigenerational Bonds. Journal of Marriage and Family, 63(1), 1-16.

4. Putnam, R. D. (2000). Bowling Alone: The Collapse and Revival of American Community. Simon & Schuster.

5. Ryff, C. D., & Singer, B. (2008). Know Thyself and Become What You Are: A Eudaimonic Approach to Psychological Well-Being. Journal of Happiness Studies, 9(1), 13-39.

6. Kram, K. E. (1985). Mentoring at Work: Developmental Relationships in Organizational Life. University Press of America.

7. McAdams, D. P. (1993). The Stories We Live By: Personal Myths and the Making of the Self. William Morrow.

8. Kaplan, M. S., & Sanchez, M. (2014). Intergenerational Programs: Support for Children, Youth, and Elders in Japan. Springer Publishing Company.

9. Rogers, C. R. (1961). On Becoming a Person: A Therapist's View of Psychotherapy. Houghton Mifflin.

10. Clutterbuck, D. (2004). Everyone Needs a Mentor: Fostering Talent in Your Organization. Chartered Institute of Personnel and Development.

11. Goleman, D. (1995). Emotional Intelligence: Why It Can Matter More Than IQ. Bantam Books.

12. Fivush, R. (2008). Remembering and Reminiscing: How Individual Lives are Constructed in Family Narratives. Memory Studies, 1(1), 49-58.

13. Harvard Business Review. (2014). The Best Mentoring Programs Know That It's a Two-Way Street. Harvard Business Review.

14. Larkin, E., & Newman, S. (1997). Intergenerational Programs: Imperatives, Strategies, Impacts, Trends. Haworth Press.

15. Schachter, S., & Singer, J. (1962). Cognitive, Social, and Physiological Determinants of Emotional State. Psychological Review, 69(5), 379-399.

16. Berkman, L. F., & Glass, T. (2000). Social Integration, Social Networks, Social Support, and Health. In L. F. Berkman & I. Kawachi (Eds.), Social Epidemiology. Oxford University Press.

Chapter 9: The Path Forward

1. Kram, K. E. (1985). Mentoring at Work: Developmental Relationships in Organizational Life. University Press of America.

2. Knowles, M. S. (1975). Self-Directed Learning: A Guide for Learners and Teachers. Association Press.

3. Putnam, R. D. (2000). Bowling Alone: The Collapse and Revival of American Community. Simon & Schuster.

4. Rogers, C. R. (1961). On Becoming a Person: A Therapist's View of Psychotherapy. Houghton Mifflin.

5. Tapscott, D. (2009). Grown Up Digital: How the Net Generation is Changing Your World. McGraw-Hill.

6. Harvard Business Review. (2014). The Best Mentoring Programs Know That It's a Two-Way Street. Harvard Business Review.

7. Diamond, P. A., & Orszag, P. R. (2005). Saving Social Security: A Balanced Approach. Brookings Institution Press.

8. Affairs.

9. Goleman, D. (1995). Emotional Intelligence: Why It Can Matter More Than IQ. Bantam Books.

10. Erikson, E. H. (1963). Childhood and Society. Norton.

11. Schwab, K. (2016). The Fourth Industrial Revolution. Crown Business.

Glossary of Terms

Attachment Theory: A psychological model describing the dynamics of long-term interpersonal relationships between humans.

Authenticity: The quality of being genuine and transparent, highly valued by digital natives in personal interactions and online presence.

Baby Boomers: Individuals born between 1946 and 1964, known for their wealth accumulation and experience in various industries.

Civil Rights Movement: A social movement in the 1950s and 1960s in the United States aimed at ending racial discrimination and promoting equal rights for African Americans.

Cognitive Development: The construction of thought processes, including remembering, problem-solving, and decision-making, from childhood through adolescence to adulthood.

Collaboration Software: Digital tools designed to help teams work together, share information, and manage projects effectively.

Collaborative Spaces: Environments, both physical and virtual, designed to encourage teamwork and the exchange of ideas among participants.

Community Investment Projects: Initiatives that involve community members in local economic development, often through collaborative efforts and shared resources.

Creative Problem-Solving: The process of finding innovative solutions to challenges by thinking outside traditional frameworks and utilizing diverse perspectives.

Cross-Generational Team: A group composed of members from different generations, leveraging diverse perspectives and experiences.

Cultural Diversity: The presence of multiple cultural groups within a society, each with its own distinct norms, values, and traditions.

Cultural Inclusivity: Creating environments where diverse cultural backgrounds and perspectives are respected, valued, and integrated into communal activities.

Digital Natives: Individuals born or brought up during the age of digital technology, familiar with computers, the internet, and smartphones from an early age.

Digital Tools: Software and applications used to enhance communication, productivity, and collaboration in a digital environment.

Diversity: The inclusion of individuals from different backgrounds, experiences, and perspectives within a group or organization.

Echo Chamber: An environment in which a person encounters only beliefs or opinions that coincide with their own, often reinforced by technology and social media.

Economic Interdependence: The mutual reliance between groups or generations for goods, services, resources, and knowledge.

Emotional Intelligence (EI): The ability to recognize, understand, and manage one's own emotions, as well as the emotions of others.

Empathy: The ability to understand and share the feelings of another person.

Flexibility: The ability to adapt to new circumstances and provide options for different ways of working or learning, appreciated by digital natives.

Generation X: Individuals born between 1965 and 1980, known for their adaptability and leadership in the workforce.

Generation Z: Individuals born from 1997 onwards, characterized by their digital fluency and social responsibility.

Generational Identity: The unique set of characteristics, values, and behaviors that define a generation, influenced by the socio-political and economic context of their formative years.

Global Awareness: Understanding and being conscious of global issues and events, facilitated by the internet and social media.

Globalization: The process by which businesses or other organizations develop international influence or start operating on an international scale.

Great Depression: A severe worldwide economic downturn that lasted from 1929 to 1939, significantly impacting the silent generation.

Inclusivity: Creating environments where all individuals feel respected, valued, and able to contribute fully.

Inclusive Financial Policies: Financial policies that support the needs of all generations, such as affordable education loans and retirement plans.

Innovation: The process of developing new ideas, products, or methods that bring value and drive progress.

Intergenerational Activities: Activities that involve participants from different generations working together or sharing experiences.

Intergenerational Bonds: Emotional and psychological connections between individuals of different generations, often involving mutual support and understanding.

Intergenerational Collaboration: Cooperative efforts between different generations aimed at leveraging diverse skills, experiences, and perspectives for mutual benefit.

Intergenerational Dialogue: Conversations between different generations aimed at sharing experiences, values, and perspectives to foster mutual understanding and respect.

Intergenerational Learning: Educational programs and practices that facilitate learning experiences between different age groups.

Intergenerational Mentorship: A relationship where older individuals guide younger ones, sharing knowledge and experience.

Knowledge Transfer: The process by which experienced individuals share their expertise with less experienced individuals.

Lifelong Learning: The continuous pursuit of knowledge and skills throughout an individual's life.

Mentorship: A developmental relationship in which a more experienced or knowledgeable person helps guide a less experienced or knowledgeable person.

Mentorship Programs: Structured relationships where experienced individuals guide and support less experienced individuals, fostering mutual learning and growth.

Millennials: Individuals born between 1981 and 1996, known for their technological prowess and entrepreneurial spirit.

Multitasking: The ability to manage multiple tasks simultaneously, a common skill among digital natives due to their exposure to various digital platforms.

Narrative Psychology: A psychological approach that views human beings as storytellers and studies how stories shape individuals' identities and actions.

Open Communication: Encouraging honest, transparent dialogue where individuals feel safe to express their thoughts and feelings.

Personal Computers: Computers designed for use by an individual, with early adoption significantly influencing Generation X and later generations.

Problem-Solving: The process of identifying solutions to specific challenges or obstacles.

Psychological Well-Being: A state of mental health that encompasses emotional stability, life satisfaction, and a sense of purpose.

Reciprocal Relationship: A relationship where each party provides benefits to the other, often involving mutual exchange and support.

Remote Work: The practice of working from a location outside the traditional office environment, enabled by digital technology.

Resilience: The capacity to recover quickly from difficulties; the ability to spring back into shape after facing adversity.

Reverse Mentorship: A mentorship model where younger individuals mentor older individuals, typically on new technologies and modern practices.

Retirement Funds: Financial systems designed to provide income to individuals after they retire from active work.

Secure Attachment: A stable and healthy emotional bond between a child and caregiver, characterized by trust and a sense of safety.

Shared Responsibility: The distribution of tasks and accountability among team members to achieve common goals.

Silent Generation: Individuals born between 1928 and 1945, whose values were shaped by the Great Depression and World War II, emphasizing hard work, resilience, and loyalty.

Social Activism: Efforts to promote, impede, direct, or intervene in social, political, economic, or environmental reform with the desire to make changes in society.

Social Cohesion: The bonds that bring society together, fostering trust, cooperation, and mutual support among its members.

Social Connectivity: The state of being connected with others through social media and other digital platforms, a hallmark of digital natives.

Social Media Platforms: Online platforms that enable users to create and share content or participate in social networking, facilitating cultural exchange.

Social Responsibility: The ethical framework which suggests that individuals and organizations should act for the benefit of society at large, strongly embraced by digital natives.

Stereotypes: Oversimplified and fixed ideas or perceptions about a group of people, often leading to misunderstandings and biases.

Story Sharing: An activity where individuals share personal stories to foster understanding, empathy, and connection across different generations.

Storytelling: The act of sharing stories, often used in families to transmit cultural heritage and life lessons across generations.

Synergy: The enhanced effect or outcome that results when individuals or groups work together cooperatively.

Technological Fluency: Proficiency in using digital technologies, which includes quickly learning and adapting to new digital tools and platforms.

Technological Proficiency: The skill and ability to effectively use and adapt to new technologies, often characteristic of younger generations.

Technology Integration: The process of incorporating new technologies into existing systems and practices to enhance productivity.

Telemedicine: The use of digital technology to deliver healthcare services and consultations remotely.

Transparency: Open and honest communication, ensuring that information is accessible and clear, valued by digital natives in both personal and professional contexts.

Trust: Firm belief in the reliability, truth, ability, or strength of someone or something.

Virtual Museums: Online platforms that provide digital access to museum collections and exhibitions, preserving and sharing cultural heritage.

Wisdom: The quality of having experience, knowledge, and good judgment, often accumulated over time and through various life experiences.

Workforce Productivity: The efficiency and output of workers in the labor force, often enhanced by collaboration and technology.

Workplace Diversity: The inclusion of individuals from various generations and cultural backgrounds within a work environment, enhancing creativity and problem-solving.

Youth Empowerment: Initiatives aimed at providing young people with the skills, opportunities, and support they need to succeed and contribute to society.

NOTES:

www.ingramcontent.com/pod-product-compliance
Lightning Source LLC
Chambersburg PA
CBHW060235030426
42335CB00014B/1468